Promoting Early Language and Literacy Development

Striving to Achieve Reading Success

Edited by
Norris M. Haynes

UNIVERSITY PRESS OF AMERICA,® INC.
Lanham • Boulder • New York • Toronto • Plymouth, UK

Copyright © 2008 by
University Press of America,® Inc.
4501 Forbes Boulevard
Suite 200
Lanham, Maryland 20706
UPA Acquisitions Department (301) 459-3366

Estover Road
Plymouth PL6 7PY
United Kingdom

All rights reserved
Printed in the United States of America
British Library Cataloging in Publication Information Available

Library of Congress Control Number: 2008924922
ISBN-13: 978-0-7618-4053-4 (paperback : alk. paper)
ISBN-10: 0-7618-4053-2 (paperback : alk. paper)

∞™ The paper used in this publication meets the minimum
requirements of American National Standard for Information
Sciences—Permanence of Paper for Printed Library Materials,
ANSI Z39.48—1984

Contents

Acknowledgments		v
1	An Overview of Early Language and Literacy Development *Nancy Marano and Norris M. Haynes*	1
2	Early Literacy Environments *Maureen Ruby and Norris M. Haynes*	16
3	Developmental Supervision: Case Studies *Maureen Ruby*	43
4	Scaffolding Early Literacy Development *Janet Price and Norris M. Haynes*	71
5	Professional Development *Nancy Marano*	82
6	Evaluation Study of Striving to Achieve Reading Success (Project STARS) *Norris M. Haynes with Michael Ben-Avie, Joy Fopiano, Maureen Gilbride-Redman, Susan Tiso, Nnandi Ihuegbu*	108
Index		149

Acknowledgments

The editor and contributors acknowledge the significant and invaluable contributions and support of the following groups and individuals:

- The Center for Community and School Action Research at Southern Connecticut State University
- Paul Flinter, Camille Jackson and Gerri Rowell of the Connecticut State Department of Education
- Julie Hirschler and Joanne Brady of the Education Development Center (EDC)
- The Staff of Connecticut Chart A Course (CCAC)
- Staff members in central offices and schools and classrooms in participating priority school districts in Connecticut
- Faculty in the School of Education at Southern Connecticut State University

Chapter One

An Overview of Early Language and Literacy Development

Nancy Marano and Norris M. Haynes

INTRODUCTION

Literacy learning and instruction has for decades captured the interest of researchers, literacy scholars, educators, and policy makers, while providing fertile ground for controversy (National Reading Panel, 2000; Snow, Burns, & Griffin, 1998). During the last five years, early literacy development has been under particular scrutiny and taken on critical significance as researchers have concluded that children's language and literacy abilities by the end of kindergarten are indeed sound predictors for children's continuing reading, and thus, academic success in later grades. As a result of national and state efforts to better align practice with research (Connecticut State Department of Education, 2000), policy makers and educators have been focusing on the needs of younger and younger children.

In this context, the focus of this book is effective early literacy development. We have included here our insights into what we have learned from the research and theoretical literature; what we have learned from the Striving to Achieve Reading Success (STARS) Projects, a professional development program of study conducted for preschool teachers and their supervisors over four years (2001–2005); and finally, what we propose as the essential elements for effective early literacy development.

For example, there is a great deal to be learned from our experiences with teaching, learning, and schooling in Connecticut. The intense focus on the learning gap between minority/low SES students in urban areas and students in wealthy suburban areas has provoked policy makers, lawmakers, education researchers and practitioners to investigate and propose ways to close that gap. This interest is especially prevalent in Connecticut where the gap in achievement between these two groups of children is dramatic. Early childhood programs, especially in "priority districts" in Connecticut, have been studied. Professional development programs have been initiated in the hopes of enriching language and literacy experiences in the early childhood educational settings in cities such as New Haven, New Britain, Bridgeport, and Meriden, all cities that have been deemed to be priority districts. Priority districts were identified in 1983 by Connecticut's State Board of Education and were defined as school districts that had significant academic need. These school districts, comprised of low income students and their families, were often in high poverty urban communities. Often the schools located in these communities evidenced a lack of excellence and educational equity. Specific goals were targeted and grants were allocated to the districts to improve the quality of teaching and learning. Various initiatives such as lowering the dropout rate, promoting early reading intervention, enhancing the use of technology, strengthening parent participation, and helping schools where necessary to obtain accreditation from the New England Association of Schools and Colleges, were implemented.

The introduction begins with an overview of the literature on early language and literacy development. We then investigate new approaches to early language and literacy development, including Connecticut's early literacy initiative. Finally, we discuss, in general, the effective elements necessary to foster early literacy development in preschools

APPROACHES TO EARLY LANGUAGE AND LITERACY DEVELOPMENT

Much of the literature on early literacy has suggested that productive literacy learning contexts are those that provide environments rich in literacy and language. In these settings, children are surrounded by—immersed in—books and language. All that they see, speak about, feel, hear, and touch facilitates the use and development of language. For example, dramatic play or art should provide every chance for conversation, for exploring through language what children are doing, thinking, imagining at any given moment. Tools and opportunities for functional writing should be included everywhere—clipboards with paper and writing tools in the dramatic play area and in the science area. Children witness very early that language and literacy (reading, writing, listening, speaking) serve many purposes in their lives. Rich literacy learning contexts are filled with occasions for children and adults to explore oral language: to ask questions, to converse, to play, to sing, to listen, to think.

To consider effective literacy learning contexts is to first examine what we mean by learning "context." Learning contexts reflect the learning process, a complex human action, and are much more than a *place* where learning happens. Rather because learning itself is multidimensional and dynamic, the learning context is a fully integrated *activity setting* (see Leont'ev, 1979; Wertsch, 1998) comprised of interdependent features, each essential to learning, yet inseparably linked to the unfolding learning process. In other words, these interacting features are essentially the relationships between and among the *who, what, where, why,* and *when* of a particular setting or event (see Vygotsky, 1978). A learning context, then, is more than the sum of its parts.

Using the perspective of activity setting enriches our understanding of context when applying the early literacy research to literacy learning. Activity settings are multidimensional, as is learning, and as proposed by Gallimore and Goldenberg (1993), effective, rich emergent literacy contexts can be best understood using the construct of activity setting. Specifically, as described by the authors, there are several contributing parts, or variables, within an activity setting: *people* who participate in the activity (children and adults and the personalities they bring); shared cultural *values* (beliefs about the importance and significance of what they are doing); task demands of the *activity* (i.e. challenges, interest level); *scripts* for the behavior of the participants (accepted and expected practices); *purposes* of the participants (goals and objectives of those involved) (p. 316). In this study of young children in emergent literacy activity settings, Gallimore and Goldenberg (1993) found that the most important influence in the development of early literacy development came from meaningful experiences with texts (p. 317), and that "... the most critical component in most emergent literacy activities is the personnel present. Someone has to be available and capable of assisting a child if we are to see 'literacy-promoting' interactions (p. 323)." In addition, the purpose of the event must be clear to the adult and the appropriate "script" or behavior will then be determined by the purpose. From our work in Project STARS we would agree with these findings, and would stress the need for a shared understanding of "meaningful experiences with texts" and of the ways we can aid caregivers and preschool teachers to support "literacy promoting interactions." All the components, and the variables, effectively facilitated and with appropriate support, are essential.

When we design and implement literacy and language activities for young children, we are reminded, as many scholars have theorized, that "cognition develops as part of an integral system in connection with motivation, affect, and values" (Minick, Stone, & Forman, 1993, p. 7). Rogoff and her associates' (1993) cross cultural study of guided participation in which children and their caregivers from two different communities were observed interacting in teaching and learning activities further supports this thinking:

> The mutual roles played by caregivers and children in children's development rely on both the caregivers' interest in fostering mature skills and the children's own eagerness to participate in adult activities and push their own development. Guided participation involves children's participation in the activities of their community with the challenge and support of a system of social partners including caregivers and peers of varying levels of skill and status. (p. 249)

In a study investigating "quality classrooms," what we would call rich literacy contexts, Dickinson and Sprague (2002) discovered that one important aspect of such classrooms was the provision for thoughtful conversation between adults and children. However, the authors explain that in order for the talk between adults and children to be beneficial and supportive of children's developing language, especially receptive vocabulary, this kind of conversation must have the properties of, as the authors describe it, "extended discourse." Extended discourse refers to discussions that are engaging, authentic, and inviting enough to provoke rich and imaginative responses in place of adult questions prompting one or two word responses. Extended discourse is open ended. Its subject matter goes beyond the here and now as adults prompt children to talk about experiences, make connections between what they know or have experienced, and new ideas to which they are being introduced. In these discussions, young children are challenged to think and talk about yesterday, today, and tomorrow as they construct meaning about their experiences while developing language as a tool to build understanding. By contributing to conversations that are open to possibility, yet connected to experience and knowledge, the participants enter into the world of imagination and abstract thought. Dickinson and Sprague (2002) found that rich literacy environments, classrooms that reflect quality, provide plenty of productive opportunities for this kind of oral language use. They discovered that language experiences in the preschool programs they studied influenced the vocabulary and early literacy development of children from low SES families. Moreover, the authors, noting that oral language development in the preschool years had lasting effects on reading achievement, conclude, "The analyses of data from all of the studies we have conducted consistently demonstrate associations among language and print-based tasks and our longitudinal data indicate that these associations continue to be strong over time" (p. 276).

We have learned that many of the most powerful occasions for promoting oral language are through shared book reading with an accompanying conversation by adults to scaffold the meaning making of the narrative. Through talk, adults and children can travel into the world the narrator has created, and respond to it in their own words, while relating the story to their own lives. Quality classrooms, as rich (literacy) learning contexts, are supportive of oral language in many ways. In addition to shared book reading, oral language and vocabulary are developed in young children through discussions about shared activities, either before, during or after those experiences have unfolded. Certainly writing, dramatic play, and singing can be incorporated into these approaches to extended discourse.

To summarize, rich learning contexts for language and literacy development are not very different from rich learning contexts in general. Because learning is a complex and multidimensional human action, we can understand the learning context as comprised of many interrelated variables that, as a result of their interactions, support and mediate learning. From this conceptual frame, the unit of study is the learning context and all of its component features: the interrelationships between and among the personnel, the children, the physical setting, the activities, the shared beliefs and values about literacy, and the purposes of specific literacy events. Furthermore, the role of the teacher as facilitator of the variables, while a variable itself is an important consideration that adds to the complexity of the design of professional development activities. Teacher learning is critically significant to enriching the learning lives of young children. Thus, professional development experiences should provide teachers not only with support in advancing their knowledge of research-based early literacy and language development, but it must also make salient the rationale for designing, implementing, and contributing to rich learning contexts that foster emergent literacy.

NEW APPROACHES TO EARLY LANGUAGE AND LITERACY DEVELOPMENT

Thanks to the work of the National Reading Panel (2000), the National Research Council (Snow, Burns, & Griffin, 1998) and David Dickinson and his associates (Dickinson, 2001; Dickinson, Miller, & Anastaspoulos, 2000; Dickinson & Sprague, 2002) researchers, scholars, and practitioners have considerably enriched their understanding of the contexts for early language and literacy development.

CONNECTICUT'S EARLY LITERACY INITIATIVE

School Readiness

In the latter half of the last decade, educators and policy makers took great interest in the physical and cognitive development of young children and the critical importance of fostering early literacy and early reading instruction. Educators and policymakers alike were concerned with the discrepant reading achievement between children from low-income urban families and their peers in schools in the suburbs, and began implementing programs to close the achievement gap. Responding to robust research studies that suggested that children's academic success is at least partly determined by their early childhood experiences before entering kindergarten (School Readiness and Child Day-Care program, www.state.ct.us/sde/), the state of Connecticut established the School Readiness and Child Day-Care program with provisions from Public Act 97-259 (An Act Concerning School Readiness and Child Day Care) in 1997. The program, a collaboration among the state Departments of Education and Social Services as well as the Department of Public Health, Children and Families, and Higher Education, was made available to priority school districts and municipalities with at least one severe-need school for children from low-income families. The purpose was to provide programs to enrich the health and experiences of young children prior to their entering the formal educational system.

In 1998, the International Reading Association (IRA) and the National Association for the Education of Young Children (NAEYC) issued a joint position statement (National Association for the Education of Young Children, 1998) regarding young children's developing literacy and language learning. In this paper, the IRA and NAEYC suggest to parents and teachers literacy practices that are developmentally appropriate for young children. These phases of development, in turn, can form a framework for designing and refining rich, supportive, and meaningful language and literacy contexts for young children. The following are the ages and experiences recommended in the joint statement: 1) preschool—awareness and exploration, 2) kindergarten—experimental reading and writing, 3) first grade—early reading and writing, 4) second grade—transitional reading and writing, and 5) third grade—conventional reading and writing (p. 1).

The National Research Council (Snow, Burns, Griffin, 1998) convened a panel of literacy experts to review research on early literacy development and reading instruction. In their analysis, these experts suggest the critical literacy learning experiences necessary to foster growth and forestall reading problems. Three key literacy events are considered essential to the foundation of young children's developing reading. First, adult-child shared book reading accompanied by rich and meaningful conversation will support vocabulary development and an understanding of concepts of print. Before children can learn to read conventionally, they must understand how a book "works." Concepts of print include such understandings as knowledge of what a word is, and what it looks like (that each word in a text is separate). While reading with their caregivers, teachers, or family members, young children discover that sentences are read from the left side of the page to the right side. In these shared reading experiences they find out that books are filled with meaning. They learn what a title is and where it is located as well as the place for the author's and illustrator's names. Children learn about punctuation marks and their general purpose in conveying meaning. In addition, receptive vocabulary, those words children understand because they have been frequently used in their presence either through book reading or through conversations with adults, helps children make sense of the stories.

Second, opportunities are created for children to develop insight into the phonology of spoken language (that words are made up of combinations of sounds). Games that involve rhyming and chorusing of favorite poems, and singing and playing with words in many different ways, create a playful sense of the ways our language works.

Third, specific activities are designed and introduced to highlight the connections between print and speech (p. 320). Shared reading of a big book where the adult or child points to each word as it is read is a good example of connecting print and speech. It also supports children's understanding of the concept of a word, where it begins, and where it ends. A variety of writing activities, including dictation, lend themselves to making the connections between print and speech. In addition, the report stresses: "Failure to develop an adequate vocabulary, understanding of print concepts, or phonological awareness during the preschool years constitutes some risk for reading difficulties" (p. 320).

Based on the recommendations from the IRA, the NAEYC, and the National Research Council, the Connecticut State Department of Education created a document meant for preschool teachers and families outlining the essential understandings about early literacy learning with suggestions for design and use in preschool settings. This document accessed on the Early Literacy website, a link on the Connecticut State Department of Education web page (Connecticut State Department of Education), also offers suggestions from the findings of the work of Teale and Sulzby (1989). These researchers explain that the following ideas are critical to a deep understanding of emergent literacy development:

- Learning to read and write begins early for children in a literate society. Children learn about literacy and authentic uses of books and writing before they learn to read and write conventionally. Children experience literacy as a purposeful activity by observing the world around them beginning very early in their lives.
- The functions of literacy are integral to the literacy learning process. A genuine purpose for the learning essential to literacy, or any kind of learning. Children observe quite early that literacy has many functions in our society. At home or at preschool, children share in activities such as: writing shopping

lists and taking them along to the grocery store; writing a friend or relative's telephone number; leaving a note for a family member; writing and sending an email; drawing a diagram or map to explain something. Children observe and experience important functions of reading: traffic signs, signs at the mall, and signs on restaurants. (By "reading" various logos that carry significant meaning in their lives.) In this way, children learn that the signs and symbols in their surrounding culture convey meaning.

- Reading, writing, and speaking are interrelated and develop simultaneously. Literacy is comprised of all aspects of expressive and receptive meaning making, and the components are reciprocal. For example, children's writing enhances their developing understanding of the printed word and phoneme awareness. Speaking reinforces all aspects of language through sound and receptive vocabulary.
- Children must actively engage with written language as they construct an understanding of how literacy works. Invented spelling, a form of experimental spelling children try out as they write and learn to match the sounds with the letters, has been shown to have a solid connection to the continued development of phoneme awareness, and later, word analysis and decoding (Morris et al, 2003).

The Early Literacy document stresses: "Early childhood teachers should be facilitators of children's existing literacy knowledge, supporting and extending it to greater levels of complexity" (p. 3), and suggests ways to foster literacy in preschool settings. Included in their suggestions are descriptions of quality learning environments for children supported by research. Preschool settings should be literacy rich. A literacy rich early childhood setting is one in which children's play is used to facilitate literacy, the physical setting fosters literacy, reading and writing is part of the daily routine, children are encouraged to read and write to each other, there are consistent and numerous shared read aloud experiences, and parents and family members are invited to engage in literacy events (pp. 3–6). Thus, responding to the research and scholarship regarding the critical relationship between early literacy and language experiences and later reading success, the Connecticut State Department of Education explicitly supports a provision for school readiness for all children, but particularly for low-income children in priority districts.

Early Reading Success

In 1998–99, extending the work already begun for preschool youngsters, the Connecticut State Assembly enacted Public Act 99-227 that provided for a statewide Early Reading Success Institute (ERSI). The Institute was accompanied by the formation of an Early Reading Success Panel whose mission included assessing reading instruction needs of priority school districts and creating a professional development plan for these districts based on the panel's recommendations (Connecticut State Department of Education, 2000). *Connecticut's Blueprint for Reading Achievement* contained the results of the panel's study and its recommendations, including explanations of the importance of oral language as a foundation for reading, and a detailed description of the curriculum for a comprehensive reading instruction program. In addition, the Blueprint outlined the necessary literacy competencies for teachers and for learners for each grade level, Kindergarten through Grade Three. In addition, the ERSI was enacted for the dissemination of the Blueprint's findings among teachers in Connecticut. The Institute collaborated with the Connecticut State Department of Education, members of the Regional Education Service Centers, district literacy coordinators, school principals, and other staff, including K-3 classroom teachers. The primary mission of the Institute was to support teachers in learning about the Blueprint and its research premise, and to acquire the knowledge base necessary for designing learning contexts that foster comprehensive reading instruction. As a result of this professional development program, teachers would have a useful guide to learner competencies for literacy at all the primary levels, as well as a framework of knowledge to plan meaningful instruction.

While *Connecticut's Blueprint for Reading Achievement* represents a comprehensive research-based explanation and description of reading instruction in the primary grades, it also points to the preschool years as the time for establishing oral language development as a foundation for emergent literacy. Rich oral language experiences promote and enhance phonological sensitivity and thus, phoneme awareness, and in turn, support the developing knowledge of meaningful vocabulary (Watson, 2002; Dickinson & Sprague, 2002). The report from the Early Reading Success Panel, in regard to directing the work of the primary grades, made salient two additional requirements: 1) the design and construction of learning contexts that foster literacy and language development for young children, and 2) a provision for professional development for early childhood educators and caregivers to learn about the importance of these contexts and ways to create them.

PROJECT STARS: THREE STRATEGIES

Overview

Striving to Achieve Reading Success (STARS): Connecticut's Early Childhood Educator Professional Development Initiative is the project at the center of this report. As part of a grant from The United States Department of Education, Project STARS has as one of its foci a professional development program that advances the knowledge and thinking of in-service early childhood educators and caregivers. The purpose of this initiative, a collaborative effort by the Connecticut State Department of Education, the Education Development Center in Newton, Massachusetts, Connecticut Charts-A-Course (CCAC), the State Education Resource Center (SERC) and the Center for Community School Action Research (CCSAR) of Southern Connecticut State University (the project evaluation team), was to provide a coordinated approach to the learning of early childhood educators from Bridgeport, Meriden, New Britain, and New Haven while supporting their career development. The project goals were first, to promote the early language and literacy development of children in order to support their success when they enter school; and second, to ensure that instruction in early language and literacy development offered in pre-service teacher preparation programs is research-based.

Thus, the state and federal governments have recognized the need for knowledgeable teachers and caregivers who can create, design, and support rich literacy learning contexts for the youngest children in Connecticut's priority districts. Connecticut has vast socioeconomic contrasts that are the source of equally contrasting academic achievement and equitable learning opportunities. To respond to these dramatic differences, the state has set goals to improve the achievement of children who live in communities where they may be considered at risk for school failure, priority districts. Thanks to the education department's School Readiness and Early Reading Success programs, more young children are receiving care that responds to their learning and developmental needs. As an extension to the programs already in place and to further support early literacy development in young children, the state enacted Project STARS to build the knowledge base for early childhood educators and their supervisors at preschool centers in priority districts. There were three primary strategies for accomplishing the goals of Project STARS: 1) Implementation of the Literacy Environment Enrichment Program (LEEP) Institute, a professional development program designed for preschool teachers and their supervisors; 2) Introduction of a literacy strand in Connecticut Charts-a-Course, a teacher learning program for early childhood caregivers who have not yet received their CDA (Child Development Associate) certificate; and 3) Establishment of a Higher Education Faculty Institute, a program designed to bring teacher educators up to date on the early literacy learning research. In an effort to offer exemplary teacher preparation programs in early literacy learning, this institute, under the auspices of the Special Education Resource Center (SERC), provided presentations and workshops given by national experts in the fields of child development and early literacy to teacher educators from various colleges and universities in Connecticut.

The First Strategy: Literacy Environment Enrichment Program (LEEP)

Literacy Environment Enrichment Program is a professional development program designed by researchers and practitioners at EDC's Center for Children and Families for early childhood teachers and their supervisors. Developed with funding from the U.S. Department of Health and Human Services, the U.S. Department of Education, the Spencer Foundation, LEEP is based on research investigations of children's language development, early literacy learning, and effective models of supervision.

The curriculum for the institute is informed by the work of David Dickinson and his associates (see Dickinson, D.K., 2001; Dickinson, D.K., Miller, C.M. & Anastaspoulos, L.P., 2000). According to Dickinson, the LEEP program takes a neo-Vygotskian perspective (Minick, Stone & Forman, 1993, cited in Dickinson & Sprague, 2002) or sociocultural perspective that views the interaction among the components of a dynamic learning context as key to fostering learning. From this perspective, the learning process unfolds in complex, multidimensional settings mediated by various tools such as language and artifacts (Vygotsky, 1978; Wertsch, 1998).

The LEEP curriculum is also informed by the work of Cochran-Smith and Lytle (1990) who have suggested that institutional supports are necessary for teachers who are attempting to learn new instructional strategies while changing or refining their beliefs. For example, LEEP incorporates a team learning approach as teachers jointly attend the institute with their supervisors. The presence of the supervisor in the professional development is meant to encourage the institution to support teachers as they change.

The work of the LEEP course is about teacher learning and improving the literacy and language development of children. As is the case with all learners, a supportive, dynamic, and meaningful learning context is essential for teacher learning. Teacher learning is defined as teachers building on their knowledge and refining their pedagogical understandings and beliefs regarding developmentally appropriate activities to foster the emergent literacy for of young children (Showers, 1990; Shulman, 1986). Teachers as learners expand their knowledge base through individual and collaborative activities, a shared discourse, self-assessment, analytical observations, and reflection (Cochran-Smith, 1991; Zeichner & Liston, 1996). The complexity of teacher learning is an important consideration in the analysis and interpretation of both teacher learning outcomes of the LEEP course, and outcomes of the children's literacy and language development.

The LEEP course, as offered by Project STARS, was a four-credit college level course with both a graduate and undergraduate credit option available to students. For participants in Project STARS, credit was offered through both Southern Connecticut and the University of Connecticut. Students signed up for and attended the course in teams of two: a preschool teacher and the center supervisor. While teachers and supervisors learned much of the same literacy-related content, LEEP sessions periodically divided participants into affinity groups so that the instructor was able to delve more deeply into classroom practices and to give supervisors opportunities to learn specific strategies to support their teachers as they adopted new practices. Assignments were performance-based and were differentiated according to the role of the participant. LEEP's face-to-face sessions were supplemented by supervisor cluster teams consisting of EDC LEEP instructors and professors from higher education institutions in Connecticut.

Through the LEEP course, teachers learned about early language and literacy development through activities that focused on the practices of reflection and intentionality. Teachers were asked, for instance, to audiotape, transcribe, and analyze their conversations. They were also asked to assess children's literacy, and adjust their instruction based on what they had learned (Dickinson & Sprague, 2002, p. 276).

Additionally, teachers learned about the critical role of oral language, specifically extended discourse, in the development of language and literacy in young children (Dickinson & Sprague, 2002). In their study, Dickinson and Sprague (2002) investigated how oral language, especially extended discourse, can be fostered using shared experiences especially shared book reading. Based on their findings, the researchers argue that quality classrooms are those in which oral language with extended discourse where children are encouraged to talk about what they have read together and whenever possible extend those conversations to make connections to their own experiences. Teachers and supervisors together learned strategies for recognizing and thus capitalizing on all opportunities that promote oral language, turning those opportunities into intentional literacy events in preschool programs. Creation of rich learning contexts that promote opportunities for talk and extended discourse was a major premise of the LEEP curriculum.

The Second Strategy: Connecticut Charts-A-Course's New Literacy Strand

Another strategy for Project STARS was the development and implementation of a research-based literacy "strand" of the Connecticut Charts-A-course

(CCAC) system. A strand is a curricular unit. Supported by Connecticut legislators and early childhood and school age educators, the CCAC system was first introduced in 1991. CCAC collaborates with the Connecticut State Department of Education, the Department of Social Services, and Connecticut Community Colleges. The early childhood education curriculum supports a developmental progression for the careers of early childhood professionals who are preparing for their Child Development Associate degree (CDA). The curriculum includes eight core areas of knowledge for teachers of young children: providing a safe, healthy and purposeful learning environment; learning about child growth and development; advancing children's physical and intellectual development; advancing children's social and emotional development; managing an effective program; establishing productive relationships with families; assessing children's learning and development; and advancing professionalism. Under the auspices of Project STARS, CCAC created and implemented a curricular literacy strand for pre-CDA educators.

The Third Strategy: Higher Education Faculty Institute

As the third strategy of Project STARS, the Special Education Resource Center (SERC) coordinated institutes for professors of pre-service teachers. With the overall goal to help children from priority districts become successful academically, the institute provided faculty in higher education with the current research in literacy and language development in young children. The intent was that teacher educators would, in turn, contribute to advancing the knowledge base for both pre-service and in-service teachers as well as administrators in their college and university classrooms and workshops. The institutes have included presentations and workshops given by national experts in literacy for faculty from various independent and public colleges and universities in Connecticut.

EFFECTIVE PRESCHOOL EARLY LITERACY DEVELOPMENT

This book describes in detail what the authors believe to be effective ways to foster language and literacy development in preschool children. Each chapter focuses on a critical aspect of effective language and literacy development. The next chapter considers the environments that support early literacy development. Chapter three presents how early language is developed and fostered in young bilingual learners. Chapter four illuminates the powerful role of supervisors; Developmental Supervision is considered through case studies. Chapter five describes critical ways that early literacy can be scaffolded. Chapter six includes a perspective on mentoring, and chapter eight presents the research on professional development in general and more specifically for early childhood professionals. Chapter seven highlights the evaluation approach and results from a study of Project STARS.

REFERENCES

Cochran-Smith, M. (1991). Learning to teach against the grain. *Harvard Educational Review, 61*(3), 279–310.

Cochran-Smith, M. & Lytle, S. (1990). Research on teaching and teacher research: The issues that divide. *Educational Researcher, 19*(2), 2–11.

Connecticut State Department of Education. (2000). *Connecticut's Blueprint for Reading Achievement: The report of the early reading success panel.*

Connecticut State Department of Education. Early literacy: Early literacy development: A focus on preschool. www.state.ct.us/sde/ Dickinson, D. K. (2001). Putting the pieces together: The impact of preschool on children's language and literacy development in kindergarten. In D.K. Dickinson & P.O. Tabor (Eds.), *Preparing for literacy at home and school: The critical role of language development in the preschool years.* (pp.1–5). Baltimore: Brookes.

Dickinson, D. K., Miller, C. M. & Anastaspoulos, L. P. (2000, June). *The impact of the Literacy Enrichment Environment Program on teachers, supervisors, and children.* Poster session presented at the annual conference of National Association for the Education of Young Children's National Institute for Early Childhood Professional Development, San Francisco.

Dickinson, D. & Sprague K. (2002). The nature and impact of early childhood care environments on the language and early literacy development of children from low-income families. In S. Neuman, & D. Dickinson (Eds.). *Handbook of early literacy research.* (pp. 263–280). New York: The Guilford Press.

Minick, N., Stone, C. A. & Forman, E. (1993). Introduction: Integration of individual, social, and institutional processes in accounts of children's learning and development. In Forman, E., Minick, N. & Stone, C.A., *Contexts for learning.* (pp. 3–16). New York: Oxford University Press.

Morris, D., Bloodgood, J. W., Lomax, R. G. & Perney, J. (2003). Developmental steps in learning to read: A longitudinal study in kindergarten and first grade. *Reading Research Quarterly, 38*(3), 302–323.

National Association for the Education of Young Children. (1998). *Learning to read and write: Developmentally appropriate practices for young children.* Joint position statement of the International Reading Association (IRA) and the National Association for the Education of Young Children (NAEYC), 53(4), 30–46.

National Reading Panel. (2000). *Teaching children to read.* Jessup, MD: Education Publications Center.

Showers, B. (1990). Aiming for superior classroom instruction for all children: A comprehensive staff development model. *Remedial and Special Education, 11*(3), 35–39.

Shulman, L. S. (1986). Those who understand: Knowledge growth in teaching. *Educational Researcher*, *15*(2), 4–14.

Snow, C. E., Burns, M. S., & Griffin, P. (Eds.) (1998). National Research Council. *Preventing reading difficulties in young children*. Washington, DC: National Academy Press.

Teale, W., Sulzby I (1989). Emerging literacy: New perspectives. In D. Strickland & L. Morrow, *Emerging literacy: Young children learn to read and write*. Newark, DE: International Reading Association.

Vygotsky, L. S. (1978). *Mind in society*. Cambridge, Massachusetts: Harvard University Press.

Watson, R. (2002). Literacy and oral language: Implications for early literacy acquisition. In S. Neuman, & D. Dickinson (Eds.), *Handbook of early literacy research*. (pp. 43–53). New York: The Guilford Press.

Wertsch, J. V. (1998). *Mind as action*. New York: Oxford University Press.

Zeichner, K. M. & Liston, D. P. (1996). *Reflective teaching: An introduction*. Mahwah, New Jersey: Lawrence Erlbaum Associates.

Chapter Two

Early Literacy Environments

Maureen Ruby and Norris M. Haynes

WHAT WE KNOW ABOUT THE HOME ENVIRONMENT

There is general consensus that the process of becoming literate begins at birth (Neuman & Roskos, 1993; Teale & Sulzby, 1989). When children interact, verbally and nonverbally, with both their caregivers and their environment, they are well on their way in their personal journey to achieving a high level of literacy. Once the journey begins, it never ends. Children continue to grow through experiences, experimenting in nurturing relationships, developing intentionality of language, and building a conceptual base about how the world works. Through the critical early period from birth to five, children are busy about with their essential job of learning. Through interactions and relationships with facilitating adults and a rich, supportive environment (Neuman & Roskos, 1993, Teale & Sulzby, 1989), children navigate through a fertile and language-rich, well-scaffolded terrain. The focus of this journey of development and early literacy acquisition is on learning, experimenting, and discovering. Adults and caregivers, through their interactions with children and the provision of a supportive and literacy-rich environment, allow children to assume active roles in taking risks as they explore and test (Teale & Sulzby, 1989). Adults, as facilitators, support and expand upon child-initiated learning (Vygotsky, 1978).

In their seminal work, *Meaningful Differences*, Hart and Risley (1995) report that the amount and kind of talking that parents and caregivers engage in with their young children is highly related to and often predictive of the size of their vocabularies and is associated with a variety of educational outcomes. The children with larger vocabularies, which are often associated with school achievement, most often had parents who talked more with them and used more positive tone in their responses and verbal exchanges. The language-rich environment contributes to the development of children's language and early literacy skills. In the Hart and Risley (1995) research, a relationship was shown between family income level and both language quantity and quality. What is critical, however, to early childhood educators, teachers, and policymakers in what Hart and Risley observed and recorded *is the relationship between affirmative relationships, substantial verbal exchange, vocabulary growth, and later academic achievement.* It is this information that should be a driving force in the development of early childhood programs. Regardless of the socio-economic level of the children's families, the early literacy environment can effectively provide *relationships that are affirmative, offer substantial verbal exchange, and nurture vocabulary growth.*

HOME ENVIRONMENTS

In home environments that are literacy-rich environments, parents, grandparents and other caregivers engage children in opportunities for daily reading of stories; expose children to books, magazines and other print sources; involve children in discourse that is often decontextualized; model for children and invite them into written language experiences; and provide props for creative and imaginative play that encourages and supports language use. In *Starting out right: A guide to promoting children's reading success*, Burns, Griffin, and Snow (1999) state that "for young children whose developing minds are striving to become literate, talk is essential—the more meaningful and substantive, the better" (p. 19). The conversations that young children engage in with caring adults are potentially the children's greatest source of new vocabulary words and they provide a rich springboard for the development and nurturing of new and creative ideas.

BEYOND THE HOME

In the development of high quality early childhood education, by design, there should be ongoing, systematic, planned, and responsive high quality language-mediated interactions between teachers and children and also between children and their peers. These conversation-rich "teacher:child" relationships are non-negotiable necessities, not luxuries. The role of the teacher as responsive language facilitator cannot be underestimated. Equally important is the actual "physical environment" of the early childhood classroom.

Early childhood teachers and child care workers are confronted with numerous responsibilities on an almost minute-to-minute basis throughout each day. The physical space of the early childhood classroom is regulated by a variety of licensing, health, and safety regulations and the focus of such requirements may render the role of the environment as "teacher" overlooked. Even without consideration of the direct educational importance of the environment, the impact from a purely aesthetic perspective is noteworthy. "The environment in the classroom has a profound effect on the feelings and actions of the children, their families, and the teachers. Children organize their world through the environment we provide." (Dombro, Colker, and Trister Dodge, 1997).

THREE APPROACHES AND THE ENVIRONMENT

Early childhood environments make a statement about the philosophy and foundations of the particular educational program and the beliefs and tenets of the facilitators of the program. In her article *Different Approaches to Teaching: Comparing Three Preschool Programs*, Amy Sussna Klein reviews three different types of preschool programs: Montessori, High/Scope®, and Reggio Emilia. She focuses a portion of her discussion on the role of the environment in each program.

Montessori

In the Montessori Method, begun by Maria Montessori in Italy in 1907, the environment is a well-planned and prepared set of spaces. The materials in the rooms of the Montessori School are matched to the ages of the students and the "work" of the children. These materials are didactic, highly organized, and designed so that students can learn concepts that are associated with "practical life issues" and self-help skills. Therefore, the setting is kept very "homelike" with child sized furniture and "real" materials such as glass containers for drinking and pouring. The environment is intended to be beautiful and aesthetically pleasing with fresh flowers adorning tables and classical music playing in the background. Through work-like, rather than play activities, children engage with self-correcting teaching materials that support them in dealing with errors in a supportive and controlled manner, which promotes repeated practice unlike the trial and error method.

High/Scope®

High/Scope® was founded in 1970 and was based on the work done by Dave Weikart and Connie Kamii on the Perry Preschool Project, an early (1962) longitudinal study in the field of early childhood. High/Scope® is constructivist in nature and encourages creative exploration with students subsequently engaging in pretend play. The environment in the program is highly organized, labeled, "materials rich," and is predictable with consistent posted daily schedules and routines. As stated by Sussna Klein,

> 'Plan-do-review' is another major component of the High/Scope framework. Children are encouraged to: 1) plan the area, materials, and methods they are going to work with; 2) do actually carry out their plan; and 3) review, articulate with the class-room community what they actually did during work time. The review time helps children bring closure to their work and link their actual work to their plan.

Additionally, the opportunity to "articulate" stresses the importance of oral language in summarizing thoughts, and summarizing reactions to the daily activities, for cognitive processing, as well as for social sharing. Materials are always readily available to children and they can access them independently. The purposeful planning of the environment is intended to support the students' exploration and engagement in activities and engagement with peers, in areas specifically planned and prepared for a variety of activities.

Reggio Emilia

Sussna Klein shares that "Reggio Emilia is a small town of about 130,000 people in Northern Italy. In 1991, Newsweek magazine noted that the system of 33 infant/toddler schools and preschools in Reggio Emilia were among the ten best school systems in the world." Three of the key principles involved in the Reggio Emilia approach are *cooperation, co-construction, and documentation*. Community building with *cooperation* is a central driving factor in the Reggio schools. Within the school environment, children and adults develop a community of trust that supports cooperation and collaboration among the members in the service of learning. Within this community environment, co-construction occurs. *Co-construction* is the process of working with others within the community and through exploring, questioning, discussing and interacting, actively learning in a more powerful manner than one would as an individual. Within this framework, new ideas are developed and students use language to process and refine their own and other's ideas. Perspective taking is supported and community members come to know one another in meaningful and productive ways. The teachers, known as pedagogistas, serve as educational consultants who serve to facilitate the children's "co-constructive activities." The role of the pedagogista is to listen intently to what the children are communicating through their many expressions including oral language, painting, drawing, music, dance, movement, sculpture, photography, as they explore and interact with the physical environment and each other. Through such facilitation, children demonstrate impressive levels of creative, symbolic accomplishment. The children are viewed as being competent and creative communicators via their involvement in co-construction. *Documentation* is a central concept to the Reggio Emilia approach and the environment is central to documentation. The classroom environment is not enslaved as a backdrop for decorative product, but rather is a vibrant communicative canvas that conveys and chronicles the story of the Reggio community, including the co-construction and collaborative discoveries and creations of its young members. The environment speaks through the process of *documentation*. The documentation, both the process and the products, are the languages of the children. Adorning the space of the school, the documentation beautifies the environment and connects all who enter and interact—children, staff, families, and the community.

The environment is regarded as a teacher in the Reggio Emilio approach, as it is in the Montessori approach. As such, the environment is designed, with careful planning and intention, to support the child in community building, co-construction and most specifically and fundamentally as a communicator. The child's interaction with the environment and other community members supports intellectual development on a variety of levels, honoring the child's need and ability to express his/her thinking through a variety of language modalities. In designing the early childhood environment one must always maintain an awareness of purpose as well as a consideration of aesthetics, and in doing so, scaffold the evolution of the voice of the child's thoughts.

COGNITIVE NEUROSCIENCE AND THE EARLY CHILDHOOD ENVIRONMENT

While the process of becoming literate begins at birth, brain development commences long before the child's official entry into the world. Since the advent of neuroimaging during the past 30 years, tremendous amounts of work have been undertaken in an attempt to more fully understand brain development. In 1994, the Carnegie Corporation published a report entitled *Starting Points,* which proclaimed that during the initial stages of human life, brain development was more rapid than previously believed. Furthermore, the report stated that a child's experiences in the early years could impact brain development. Early experience can affect the course of early brain development, both positively and negatively. The idea that experience, and therefore, environment, could influence brain development caught the attention of the public and policymakers, as well as the scientific community.

Following the release of *Starting Points* in 1996, Carnegie Corporation of New York and the Families and Work Institute co-sponsored a multidisciplinary conference on early brain development. One outcome of the conference was the report *Rethinking the Brain: New Insights into Early Development.* The content of the report focused on the interplay of genetics and the environment (or "nature and nurture") and the effect of this interaction on subsequent short and long-term outcomes for the individual. The report had important implications for early childhood educators as they considered the role of early childhood education environments and the concepts of early intervention, prevention, and opportunities. The critical role of early childhood educators in nurturing relationships with children was also highlighted. Considering the tremendous intellectual, emotional, and physical development children undergo in the years of early childhood (NAEYC defines "early childhood" as from Birth through 8 years of age), the report underscored the non-negotiable need to insure that enriching, nurturing environments are provided for all children during the crucial stages of development. "While learning continues throughout the life cycle, there are 'prime times' for optimal development—periods during which the brain is particularly efficient at specific types of learning" (Shore, 1997, p.39). It became clear that the early childhood environment has astounding effects on virtually every component of early development.

McCain and Mustard, in their *Early Years Study; Reversing the Brain Drain,* a study done in Canada, declared,

> We examined the evidence from the neurosciences, developmental psychology, social sciences, anthropology, epidemiology, and other disciplines about the relationship among early brain and child development and learning, behavior, and health throughout all stages of life. We consider, in view of this evidence, that the period of early child development is equal to or, in some cases, greater in importance for the quality of the next generation than the periods children and youth spend in education or post secondary education." (McCain and Mustard, 1999).

Their study and resulting recommendations support the "optimizing" of the early childhood period.

Meanwhile, concurrently in the United States, the Center for Studies of Behavior and Development, an administrative unit of the Division of Behavioral and Social Sciences and Education (DBASSE) of the National Research Council (NRC), an operating arm of The National Academies, directed the Committee on Developments in the Science of Learning, a body of sixteen key cognitive scientists from throughout the United States, to conduct a comprehensive study of developments in the field of learning sciences in the late 1990's. This committee reviewed research from developmental psychology, cognition, cognitive neuroscience, sociology, anthropology, learning, educational technology, and also the *design of educational environments*. This was an attempt to synthesize the current body of knowledge and to support the transference of research to practice. In 1999, John Bransford, Anne Brown and Rodney Cocking (1999) edited a review of the work compiled by the Committee on Developments in the Science of Learning. In their book, *How People Learn: Brain, Mind, Experience and School* (1999), they also reported findings of convergence of information from several disciplines. It was generally agreed that learning changes the anatomical structure of the brain and these structural changes can affect function.

Psychologists, cognitive scientists, neuroscientists, pediatricians, linguists, special educators, child development specialists and a variety of other stakeholders have collaborated to advance the knowledge base and to translate research to practice. Psychologist and cognitive neuroscientist Paula Tallal, Ph.D. has been involved in studies using functional magnetic resonance imaging (fMRI) as a means to locate and identify the brain regions that do not adequately process letter/sound combinations and result in students experiencing reading difficulties. The fMRI images demonstrate that children who have dyslexia show decreased activity in the area of the brain that is involved in phonological processing (language-critical left temporoparietal region). Working with colleague, Dr. Michael Merzenich, Dr. Tallal developed neuroplasticity-based computerized software activities that effectively changed the brain architecture and function of the children in their study. The areas of the brain that are required for executive reading skills began to function similarly to the brains of non-impaired children after the children participated in the treatment activities. (Temple, 2003)

Dr. Kenneth Pugh, a psychologist at Haskins Laboratories and Yale Medical School, and colleague of Drs. Sally and Bennett Shaywitz, is a leader in neuroimaging and the advancement of using research to diagnose and treat learning disabilities, including dyslexia, as well as in supporting advances in the understanding of attention and memory and the implications for teaching and learning. "We're bringing together imaging with sophisticated cognitive-behavioral work to better understand how reading failure occurs and, from this, better techniques to correct it," says Pugh. (Murray, 2000.) The work of Tallal, Merzeich, Pugh, Sally and Bennett Shaywitz and others in the areas of dyslexia and learning disabilities has critical implications for early childhood educators and caregivers. With the information we have available through consensus of research findings, society must begin to seriously focus on these findings and the implications they have for the important early years to insure that children have early learning environments and experiences in preschool that nurture their brains and prepare them for ongoing learning.

GOVERNMENT AND EARLY CHILDHOOD LEARNING

Concomitant with the reporting of scientific findings on the brain and learning, the White House began dialoguing with the public, policymakers, scientists and other interested parties regarding early childhood education. In his State of the Union Address on February 4, 1997, President Bill Clinton said,

> Learning begins in the first days of life. Scientists are now discovering how young children develop emotionally and intellectually from their very first days, and how important it is for parents to begin immediately talking, singing, even reading to their infants . . . We already know we should start teaching children before they start school.

Additionally, a White House conference, *Early Childhood Development and Learning: What New Research on the Brain Tells Us about Our Youngest Children,* was hosted by the Clintons that year. According to archived White House information, "The conference moderator was Dr. David Hamburg of the Carnegie Corporation of New York. The presenters included Dr. Carla Shatz, University of California, Berkeley; Dr. Donald Cohen, Yale Child Study Center; Dr. Patricia Kuhl, University of Washington; Dr. Ezra Davidson, Drew University of Medicine; Dr. T. Berry Brazelton, Harvard University; and Dr. Deborah Phillips, National Research Council.

Each of these individuals emphasized the importance of children's earliest experiences in helping them to get a strong and healthy start. For the first time, we saw the intricacies of the infant's brain taking shape and how rapidly that happens. This served to reinforce our beliefs about the importance of early experiences in promoting development and learning. We also saw that many activities that parents currently engage in, such as singing, talking, and reading to babies and children, improve children's ability to learn and develop throughout their lives.

The insights reported at the White House conference resulted from decades of systematic inquiry. They emerged from questions tackled by scientists and scholars and from the experiences of parents and others who have spent their days with children and families. The purpose of this inquiry was not simply to accumulate knowledge but to reach a deep understanding of how children grow and how families, communities, and the nation as a whole can contribute to the next generation's healthy development and learning.

In the foreword, written by Richard W. Riley, a statement is made regarding the Clinton Administration's investment in children and families as exemplified by the commitment to research, increased funding for Head Start and the WIC Supplemental Nutrition Program, and the creation of the Early Head Start program. Riley stated, "The White House conference is a call to action to all members of society—including health care providers, businesses, the media, faith communities, child care providers, and government, to use this vital research to strengthen America's families."

In a publication titled: *"How Are the Children?" Report on Early Childhood Development and Learning*. (White House Archive, 1999), the federal government focused on public and governmental attention on the importance of the early years in child development and learning, with special emphasis placed on 10 key lessons." These lessons are outlined in the publication as follows:

These 10 key lessons are drawn from current research on child development, and collectively form an argument for careful attention to the early years of life as critically formative. Each of the lessons introduces a piece of information about brain development in easy-to-understand terms, and explains its significance for parents and caregivers.

The 10 lessons are:

1. new brain research underscores the importance of education and the power of effort;
2. early experience affects how brains are "wired";
3. the young brain is a work in progress;
4. every child is unique;
5. children learn in the context of important relationships;
6. other caregivers can meet young children's needs, but don't take the place of mom or dad;
7. "small talk" has big consequences;
8. children need many kinds of stimulation;
9. prevention is crucial; and
10. the cradle will rock.

The overall message of the 10 key lessons is that research has shown the early years to be critical for children's healthy development. The experiences children need during those years are easily provided if we are aware of their needs and recognize the long-term significance of ongoing brain development.

The report asserts that each child born in our country arrives with billions of brain cells just waiting to have their power unlocked. Many of these cells have already begun to link up to one another, but a newborn's brain has yet to form the roughly 100 trillion connections that make up an adult's complex neural networks. For these connections to form and proliferate, cells need a crucial ingredient: experience in the world. From the very first days of life, brain cells connect at an astonishing pace. Young brains forge more than enough connections in the first 3 years of life. As children move toward adulthood, these connections are pruned and fine-tuned. This is good news for humans. It means that our newborns' capacities—their unique ways of thinking, knowing, and acting—develop in the world, under the sway of the adults who love them and nurture them.

The impact of early experience on early brain development is powerful and specific, and may last a lifetime. This is a major finding of recent brain research, and it represents a sharp departure from centuries-old ideas about how children develop and grow. Its implications can be summarized in 10 key lessons that emerged from the conference.

The nature vs. nurture contest is dealt with in lesson one of the paper. Geneticists and other scientist acknowledge the genetic blueprint we are each born with and the role that hereditary plays in development, however, we continue to learn about the effects of the environment and experience on the "blueprint." In *"How Are the Children?" Report on Early Childhood Development and Learning* (1999), it is stated that

> researchers are producing new evidence that in the early years, nurture leads that dance; one recent study suggests that in infancy and childhood, the impact of experience on cognitive ability is significantly more powerful than the influence of heredity. The relative importance of experience appears to decrease as individuals move through the life cycle ... scientists now underscore the importance of early experience, the power of effort, and the hope of education.

Lesson 2 deals with how early experience affects how brains are wired. At birth, children's brains are in a surprisingly unfinished state. Newborns have all of the genetic coding required to guide their brain development. What's more, they have nearly all of the billions of brain cells, or neurons, they will need for a lifetime of thinking, communicating, and learning. But these neurons are not yet linked up into the networks needed for complex functioning. It is like having billions of telephones installed around the nation, but not yet completely connected to each other. The extreme immaturity of the newborn's brain is uniquely human. Experience plays a far greater role in the wiring of our brains. Our developing nervous systems can be significantly altered and fine-tuned by experience. This makes humans uniquely flexible and adaptable. It also allows us to have far greater individuality than other species. Different people's brains—even those of identical twins—will be wired differently based on their responses to different activities and stimuli

Lesson 3 addresses the fact that the young human brain is a "work in progress." As discussed, the progress with the science of neuroimaging permits scientists to study the functioning brain's structures. The technology permits study of anatomy and functionality in various stages of development, including the pre and perinatal periods.

> Crucial steps in brain development take place early in pregnancy, before many women know that they are expecting. Within weeks of conception, cells that are destined to become neurons have to find their way to the correct position in the part of the brain most responsible for reasoning and learning. For brain development to proceed normally, each cell has to make its journey at the right time, in the right order. Nature has powerful mechanisms to guide the process, including genetic coding, and expectant parents can rest assured that in the vast majority of cases, development proceeds just as it should. But even in the womb, the brain is vulnerable to environmental influences. When pregnant women have inadequate nourishment, when they smoke, drink, or take drugs, or are exposed to toxic substances, their babies' brain development may be jeopardized. Research also suggests that when women suffer abuse, extreme stress, or severe depression, their babies may be affected.

From birth onward, babies have a tremendous awareness of their surroundings. Learning begins at birth. As new experiences arrive, young children's brains respond by forming and reinforcing trillions of connections, or synapses, among neurons. In the time that it takes for mom to nurse the baby or for grandpa to read *Goodnight Moon*, thousands of new synapses are produced. At the same time, thousands of existing synapses are used or "fired" and, in the process, reinforced.

Connections form so quickly that by the time children are three, their brains have twice as many synapses as they will need as adults. These trillions of synapses are competing for space in a brain that is still far from its adult size. According to *Rethinking the Brain* (Shore, 1997), a report by the Families and Work, by the age of three a young child's brain is apt to be more than twice as active as that of her pediatrician. Children are biologically primed for learning, and the first 3 years are particularly crucial. If children have more synapses than they will have as adults, what happens to the trillions of excess connections? The answer is they are shed as children grow. Scientists report that throughout the development process, the brain is producing new synapses, strengthening existing ones, and getting rid of synapses that aren't used often enough. Before the age of 3, synapse production is by far the dominant process; from 3 to 10, the processes are relatively balanced, so the number of synapses stays about the same. But as children near adolescence, the balance shifts, and the shedding of excess neurons moves into high gear.

Brains downsize for the same reasons so many other "organizations" do: with streamlined networks, they can function more efficiently. But how does the brain "decide" which connections to shed and which to keep? Here again, early experience plays a decisive role. Each time synapses fire, beginning with the early months and years of life, they get sturdier and more resilient. Those that are used often enough tend to survive; those that are not used often enough are history. In this way, a child's experiences in the first years of life affect her brain's permanent circuitry.

Lessons 4, 5, and 6 deal with the fact that every child is unique, that children learn in the context of important relationships, and that other caregivers can meet young children's needs but they don't replace parents. These three features are important and relationships within all contexts of the child's life are critical. Lessons 7 and 8—small talk has big consequences and children need many kinds of stimulation—are of paramount significance in the realm of the early childhood environment and depend upon the relationships that each unique child has within the context of these relationships.

Research, including the studies of Hart and Risley (1995), highlights the significance of early language experiences. According to the *Report on Early Childhood Development and Learning*, "more precisely, they are stressing the importance of "small talk"—the millions of ordinary greetings, exclamations, explanations, complaints, and utterances exchanged between adults and children in the course of the early years."

New research shows that infants make more rapid progress in cracking the language code than we previously thought. From their early months, they pay close attention to the language they hear. By the time they reach their first birthdays, they are well on their way to mapping the sound structure of language—or, in multilingual homes, to the language they hear most consistently.

Adults have special ways of talking to children that help them analyze language. Intuitively, they speak more rhythmically, slowing down their speech, exaggerating phonetic shifts, and simplifying their vocabulary and grammar. Speakers of "parentese" often set their words to enticing melodies that act as acoustic hooks, pulling the baby's attention to them. This kind of talk lets babies know that they are being addressed; punctuated by pauses, it helps young children learn that relating to others is about taking turns. Many kinds of early interactions—a game of peekaboo or mimicry of a baby's faces— can lay the groundwork for effective communication later in life. Not all parents are aware of the need to speak with their young children. Whatever the reasons may be for not engaging in conversations with babies and toddlers, the result is that the children miss out on significant and necessary experiences essential to language learning.

Children require stimulation beyond conversation in order to develop a variety of other abilities. They need to develop "... their powers of perception, social prowess, and aesthetic and moral capacities. And of course, all children need physical exercise. When children are severely deprived of experience in any of these areas, their development may be delayed." Studies have been done with children from orphanages who remain inactive in cribs throughout the majority of their days and they exhibit developmental delays. The *Report on Early Childhood Development and Learning* (1999) states: "Children need opportunities for vigorous, safe physical activity. They need touch, sounds, and images. They need social and emotional contact. And they need thought-provoking activities. Most adults who care for children have some awareness of these needs. But despite parents' best intentions, many infants and toddlers do not get enough intellectual stimulation. This was a major finding of *Starting Points*, a Carnegie Corporation report on meeting the needs of young children that was cited at the White House Conference. *Starting Points* reported that only half of infants and toddlers are routinely read to by their parents."

Lessons 9 and 10—prevention is crucial and the cradle will rock—deal with the absolute requirement for early intervention and prevention in all aspects of a child's life along with the need for unconditional love. As cited in the report, "... the earlier the intervention, the better; the more follow-up, the better. These are simple lessons. As they are applied more widely, results for young children are bound to improve."

POLITICAL SUPPORT FOR EARLY CHILDHOOD AND LITERACY IN THE NEW CENTURY

The White House Summit on Early Childhood Cognitive Development

After the Clinton presidency came to a close, the momentum of support for early childhood literacy in the research community and Washington did not end. Mrs. Bush, U.S. Secretary of Education Rod Paige, and U.S. Secretary of Health and Human Services Tommy Thompson hosted The July 2001 White House Summit on Early Childhood Cognitive Development. Focusing on the period of tremendous growth and change that is the hallmark of early childhood, the conference addressed what parents, grandparents, early childhood educators, childcare providers, and others could contribute in support of ensuring children had enriching and appropriate experiences. A number of other initiatives that Mrs. Bush has been associated with have focused on early childhood cognitive and literacy development, including her Ready to

Read, Ready to Learn education initiative; The Healthy Start, Grow Smart magazine series; Healthy Start, Grow Smart Publications—*Put Reading First: Helping Your Child Learn to Read* and *Put Reading First: The Research Building Blocks for Teaching Children to Read*; The New Teacher Project; Troops to Teachers; and others. (http://www.whitehouse.gov/firstlady/initiatives/education/earlychildhood.htm)

It appears that research is now supporting what we in early childhood education have been saying for years. That is, positive early experiences forge the foundations for lifelong learning and behavior. And, to optimize the development of each child, a rich nurturing environment is required (Diamond & Hopson, 1998; Fischer & Rose, 1998). Such support has been abundant in news articles and journal publications in connection with the importance of early experiences in brain development of the young child (Begley, 1997; Nash, 1997). In essence, rich environments produce rich brains and an essential agent in this process is movement activity!

Experience has been found to affect the physical structure of the brain, a phenomenon known as plasticity. The brain grows new connections with environmental stimulation (Diamond 1988) and modifies itself structurally depending on the amount and type of usage (Healy 1990). Each new stimulation and experience rewires the brain. Enriched environments enable the brain to grow more neural connections, thickening the cortex of the brain, while less stimulating environments actually have a thinning effect on the cortex (Diamond and Hopson 1998). Enriched environments provide challenge by including reading and language, motor stimulation, a focus on the arts, stimulating surroundings, and a wide variety of approaches to thinking and problem solving. Exposing children to a variety of problem solving approaches acknowledges the complexity of the brain. Children should be encouraged to explore alternative thinking, multiple answers and creative insights. It is agreed that experience structurally changes the brain, and thus, the more children are exposed to and learn, the more individualized their brains become.

Criteria for the Early Childhood Literacy Environment

Gail Lindsey, assistant director of the National Center for Rural Early Childhood Learning Initiatives and of the Early Childhood Institute at Mississippi State University, cites Simmons and Sheehan in a 1997 article as writing, "Daycare is more than a service that holds daily schedules intact. It is a place where children build their brains." (Lindsey, 1999). As evidenced by the research, this is true not only of daycare, but also preschools, homes, and any environment into which we entrust our youngest citizens. How then should we define the criteria for an appropriate early childhood literacy environment?

In considering a literacy-rich preschool environment, there are two key features: the organization of the environment and the teacher's role. The classroom environment includes the actual layout of the classroom space and the contents. The design must facilitate multiple opportunities for students to engage in activities that promote literacy and language development. As stated in the Connecticut State Department of Education document, *Early Literacy: Early Literacy Development: A Focus on Preschool.* "The physical environment must beckon children to speak, read, and write and support their natural disposition to progress as readers and writers." (http://www.state.ct.us/sde/deps/Early/literacy.pdf, p.4) Critically important, and without whom no physical space will support a child's literacy development, are the teachers who actively facilitate language activities, responding to the needs of the students and offering immediate feedback and support. "Children learn how to attend to language and apply this knowledge to literacy situations by interacting with others who model language functions." (Gunn, Simmons, & Kameenui, 1995, p.11).

The physical space, as described by Montessori and in Reggio Emilio schools, should be designed to create an inviting and comfortable environment. There should be distinct sections that are arranged for a variety of group sizes and activities. The traffic patterns within and between these spaces should be carefully planned, analyzed, and tested to insure that there are no inviting "runways" for children to practice their acceleration skills. A quiet, cozy, well-lit area where children can relax and engage in reading by themselves, with a friend, or with an adult should invite the children to become intimate with books in an authentic setting. This area can be set up much like a home living room or study with soft furnishings. A rich, warm library-like atmosphere should provide a variety of books that appeal to young children and are of different genres and reading levels. Fiction and non-fiction should be equally represented. A sizeable collection of books should be readily available and should include picture books, nursery rhymes, finger plays, poems, fantasy stories, classical children's books, traditional tales, recipes, songs, authentic literature, multicultural books, humor books, as well as books written in languages represented by the student population. Each area of the room should have books and materials and props for writing. An area dedicated specifically for writing should also be available. Clearly distinct from the art area, children can experiment with writing letters, lists, stories, creating little books, running businesses, or making journal entries. Artists and their work are in an area dedicated to painting and drawing, and a variety of creative media should be proximal to a sink, if possible, for cleanup and management. The books and writing materials within the housekeeping area, block area, reading area, science area, computer area, art area, music area, computer area, as well as all other areas should be easily and independently accessible to children. Carefully chosen, these child-appropriate books are intended to support activities that generally take place within the particular areas. For example, the kitchen area of the dramatic play center might have telephone memo pads, shopping list pads, coupons, newspapers, envelopes, stamps, cook books, phone books, etc. Books on building, maps, drawing paper, blueprints, rulers, colored pencils and a variety of craft materials to make road signs should be strategically placed in the block area. Budding artists are surrounded by class-made books of student art work where student dictated captions can be displayed, as well as books on famous artists and pictures of fine art. Observation and data collection sheets located in the science center encourage students to record what they experience and to place the sheets in a note book or science journal. Tape recorders have a variety of uses beyond playing taped books. Tape recorders can be provided so that children can record their thoughts, responses, interviews, or conversations. Children should be encouraged to use technology, beyond computers. Young photographers can learn to use cameras and the pictures can be used as story props, story starters or to complement writing. Photographs serve as records and seeds for conversations after class events and outings. Overhead projectors can be used with preschoolers to stimulate their thinking as they engage with letters, shapes, shadows, and a variety of activities.

It is important to display the work of the children in the room, as well as charts and posters made with the students during whole group discussions. The bulk of what adorns the walls of the classroom should be work that has been done directly by the children or expressly with the children. It should relate to what they are currently involved in, and actively exploring, in the curriculum. Therefore, what is displayed in the environment will be stimulating. It follows that materials displayed will change as the focus of activity changes and children's work products will not become like wallpaper, a permanent and stagnant background in the room. A print-rich environment that is comprised of work that is co-created with students is most meaningful in developing children's literacy and language skills. The teacher accesses the co-created print as an instructional tool to scaffold the children's learning. They have a connection to the print and the teacher can build upon this background in a dynamic and interactive manner. This is much more powerful than relying on purchased, pre-fabricated classroom decorations.

> The challenge for early childhood educators is to think beyond decorating to consider how walls can be used effectively as part of an educational environment. In

Reggio Emilia the walls display documentation panels of projects that children are engaged in. These become the basis of ongoing research and dialogue between the children, teachers, and families. Panels of photos, artifacts, and text make "learning visible" to participants and to outsiders. Documentation differs from display in that it includes explanatory text and children's own words, helping the viewer understand children's thinking and their processes rather than just end products. Documentation is ongoing and part of planning and assessment. It encourages children to revisit an experience and to share a memory together. It can provide opportunities for further exploration or new directions. (Tarr, 2004)

When it comes to walls and commercial materials, it is clear when considering the early literacy needs of young children, "more" does not equate to" better." The purpose of what is put up and how it directly relates to and supports student learning is of paramount consideration.

Children should not only engage in their own writing, but they should see writing modeled by their teachers and other adults. By observing teachers scripting student dictated messages and by writing language experience stories, children learn that print carries a message, that one's thoughts and experiences can be captured and recorded on paper, that the squiggles on the paper carry meaning and can be read over and over, and that directionality is important in writing a message. Writing experiences reinforce the "concepts about print" that students are becoming aware of through their book experiences.

When teachers read to children in the early literacy classroom, they are not only giving the children the gift of a good story, but they are supporting the students' development of understanding how books work. The experience teaches children about book structure, book language, "story grammar"— characterization, setting, story problems and solutions, the concepts of beginning, middle and end, and exposes children to rich, new vocabulary. The fluent reading of a story by a teacher is motivating to young children and models good "reading behavior." Reading aloud to groups or individuals also encourages the development of good listening skills. While listening to stories, chants, and poems, children are audience to new language. Teachers select materials with beautiful rhythm, rhyme, alliteration and playful language to support children's developing phonological awareness. Having heard selected stories, the children then have a common background knowledge for further experiences with guided language play. Teachers guide students to discovering and practicing with the patterns of sounds within language. This attentiveness to sounds is necessary for developing the skills needed for reading (phonemic awareness) and supporting children in tending to details in sounds and in speech.

Read alouds coupled with conversations about the text are critical to the oral language development of early learners. Since oral language is a foundation to later learning, it is in the best interest of children to provide them with multiple opportunities to develop their oral language skills. Listening to teachers read quality literature and interacting with caring, nurturing adults in conversation about the story helps children process and organize new information, develop new thoughts, verbalize new ideas, make connections to themselves and what they already know, ask questions, express feelings, and experience and harness the power of language. By exploring new ideas via the mediation and scaffolding of a teacher, children learn to respond to both literature and others. Eventually, they become more fluent in idea generation, organization, and expression. Being able to put language to ideas and feelings enhances emotional development and social language. These are essential skills in the development of good social interaction skills and healthy interpersonal relationships.

Early Literacy Environment, LEEP, and Project STARS

The early literacy environment is a focal point of the LEEP course. A quality early literacy environment is essential to the success of the early childhood experience. A mutual goal of both LEEP and Project STARS was to provide early childhood professionals with the educational experience through a college course to understand the role of the environment and the teacher in a preschool child's development of literacy skills. As a grant funded research endeavor, Project STARS sought to quantify the effects of the LEEP course on the early literacy environment and the activities and experiences children engaged in within those environments. The task of evaluating preschool environments is a daunting one; the components are many. The ELLCO, Early Language and Literacy Classroom Observation Toolkit, was chosen to be used in the study of the impact of the LEEP course on the early literacy environment.

ELLCO: Early Language and Literacy Classroom Observation Toolkit

Project STARS, in its efforts to support early childhood professionals in providing young children with both opportunities and the scaffolding to develop language and literacy skills, sought an evaluative tool for gauging the effectiveness of the project. Ideally, this tool would inform the systematic monitoring and measurement of the effects of Project STARS relative to the nature and quality of the environmental support for preschoolers' emergent literacy, the professional development and practice of the teachers, and the learning outcomes of the students. Fortunately, the State of Connecticut had previously requested assistance from the New England Comprehensive Center (NECC) for the development of an observation tool for early literacy in preschool classrooms. Through grant support from the U.S. Department of Education, the Office of Educational Research and Improvement, the Spencer Foundation, the Agency for Children and Families, and the Interagency Educational Research Initiative, and with the cooperation of NECC, the Connecticut State Department of Education, and the Waterbury Connecticut Board of Education and Educational Development Center, Inc., *Kenny's Story* was written and the *Early Language and Literacy Classroom Observation Toolkit* was developed and tested. The ELLCO was based upon a body of research in children's oral language and literacy development, including the work of David Dickinson, Catherine Snow and others. David Dickinson and Susan Neumann co-edited the *Handbook of Early Literacy Research* (Guilford Press, 2001), which presents research evidence that identifies effective foundations for cultivating emerging language and literacy in diverse preschool populations.

Kenny's Story was developed to be used as a vehicle for supporting both teachers and ELLCO observers in understanding the importance of the early childhood classroom environment and the literacy practices that occur within the environment relative to children's developing oral language and emergent literacy skills. Having Kenny's experience as a young, African American kindergartner from a priority school district as a common focus and springboard for discussion and reflection provides context for exploring the critical importance of observing, monitoring, and evaluating the literacy environment and teaching practices with a research-based tool. In the fictional narrative, Kenny comes alive as he interacts with his peers during free-choice time in his kindergarten environment. Interspersed within the vignette format of *Kenny's Story* are: a concise presentation of pertinent research on early literacy, explanations of practical application of research to classroom practice, and a summation of the implications of the importance of supporting children's emergent literacy development for administrators and policy makers. *Kenny's Story* and Chapter 5 of the *User's Guide to the Early Language and Literacy Classroom Observation Toolkit* are available online at: http://www.brookespublishing.com/ellco.

Miriam Smith, David Dickinson, Angela Sangeorge, and Louisa Anastasopoulas collaborated to develop the ELLCO Toolkit in response to the need for a research-based evaluation tool to collect data, to construct profiles, and to conduct both ongoing studies and professional development. Intended outcomes included the enhancement of student language and literacy learning, the enrichment of teacher understanding of the critical role of research-based instructional practices and the importance of the early childhood classroom environment. The toolkit consists of three separate, yet inter-reliant, components: the *Literacy Environmental Checklist*, the *Classroom Observation and Teacher Interview*, and the *Literacy Activities Rating Scale*.

As a research-based observation tool, the ELLCO Toolkit has four main uses. It can be used *by researchers* to document and monitor program implementation. It can be used systematically as a component of *school improvement* efforts. While monitoring programmatic issues that impact literacy instruction and student opportunities, student performance data can be analyzed and compared to determine programmatic impact on achievement. Principals and supervisors of early childhood programs can harness the power of the ELLCO Toolkit in their *supervisory capacity*. Without a systematic methodology for monitoring and evaluating classroom environments and practice, appropriate supports, based upon analyzed data, cannot be provided to teachers. ELLCO, when used for supervision, opens up opportunities for focused interaction between supervisors and teachers in efforts to improve teacher knowledge base with concomitant delivery of more effective researched-based support of students. This supports the fostering of emergent and developing early literacy and language skills Finally, and perhaps most importantly, ELLCO can be an effectual influence in *professional development*. When trained to utilize the toolkit in their personal practices, teachers have a common vehicle for personal and collaborative reflection. The toolkit provides a structure that supports the focusing of energy and effort on those elements of practice that are vital to student learning and programmatic success, and are readily observable by trained and informed users. By focusing on definable, observable dimensions of effective literacy environments and practice, connections can be made between research and practice to promote growth and positive change for professionals.

To use the ELLCO Toolkit, teachers, literacy coaches and/or facilitators, supervisors, and researchers should meet several prerequisites. All users of the tool should have in depth knowledge of language and literacy development during early childhood (defined as birth through eight years of age). Users should have experience in working with and teaching students from preschool through grade 3. Additionally, as a research-based tool, users should be appropriately trained by an experienced ELLCO training facilitator. During training, through the employment of *Kenny's Story*, users share in a common perspective of what defines pre-kindergarten through grade 3 research-supported literacy instruction, study the components of the tool and the accompanying scoring rubrics, and practice with the tool in simulated and live classroom situations, as well as with video-tapes. Interrater reliability is dependent upon appropriate user training. During the supervised practice portion of the training experience, trainees pair with experienced users to observe in a classroom. Interrater reliabilities have been found to average 88% for the *Literacy Environmental Checklist*, 90% and higher for the *Classroom Observation,* and 81% for the *Literacy Activities Rating Scale* (Smith and Dickinson, 2002).

In Project STARS, the principle use of ELLCO was as a research tool. Initially, the ELLCO was used to obtain baseline data of the classrooms of teachers enrolled in the four credit Literacy Environment Enrichment Program (LEEP) class, as well as in the comparison group of "non-LEEP" teachers. It was later used to measure and document any observable changes after completion of LEEP training. The information garnished from the use of ELLCO, when analyzed with measures of change in student achievement before and after LEEP participation of teachers, can yield information on the effectiveness of implementation of new strategies that enhance literacy instruction, can promote positive changes to the literacy environments, and can increase literacy learning opportunities for students. The collection of "pre" and "post" ELLCO data, when implementing new literacy programs, can yield powerful information on program strengths and challenges. The ELLCO provides for essential programmatic progress monitoring.

Prior to using the ELLCO Toolkit, the front page of the observation booklet, known as the Observation Record, is filled out by the observer(s). Data is accumulated on this document that tracks the demographics of the students in the classroom. Information including number, ages, sex, grades of students, as well as dominant classroom language, number of English language learners, number of special education students, length of day, number of teachers and other adults present, and time and date of observation is recorded. This serves not only as an important record of information, but also as a segue for the observer to connect with the classroom and the teacher(s).

The *Literacy Environmental Checklist*, the first component of the ELLCO, is an inventory-like assessment that precedes the other components. The "checklist" provides structure for the observer(s) to get a "feel" for the classroom environment in an efficient manner. By completing the 24 item survey in a typical 20 minute session, the observer becomes familiar with the blueprint and the contents of the classroom environment. An awareness of the setting of the classroom, the arrangement of the furnishings, and the organization of the available contents, primes the observer for a more intentional *Classroom Observation.* The "checklist" can easily be completed when class is not in session, either before or after students are in program or while they are not active throughout the classroom (recess, outdoor, recess, library, etc.). If need be, it can also be done while children are present.

There are five categories containing 24 items in the *Literacy Environmental Checklist:*

- Book Area (3 items)
- Book Selection (4 items)
- Book Use (5 items)
- Writing Materials (6 items)
- Writing Around the Room (6 items)

Each of the 24 items is scored, according to provided guidelines, and the five categories are subtotaled. These subtotals are then summed for a total score for the *Literacy Environmental Checklist.* When observations are done in tandem, pairs share their ratings following the observation and scoring to verify consistency (see interrater reliability).

The *Classroom Observation and Teacher Interview* consists of fourteen items. These items allow the observer to examine language and literacy practices in pre-kindergarten through grade three classrooms, while focusing on *The General Classroom Environment* (6 items) and *Language, Literacy, and Curriculum* (10 items).

The two dimensions of the *Classroom Observation* and their corresponding items are delineated as follows:

- *The General Classroom Environment*
  1. Organization of the Classroom
  2. Contents of the Classroom
  3. Presence and Use of Technology
  4. Opportunities for Child Choice and Initiative
  5. Classroom Management Strategies
  6. Classroom Climate
- *Language, Literacy, and Curriculum*
  1. Oral Language Facilitation
  2. Presence of Books
  3. Primary: Approaches to Book Reading (Pre-K and K)
  4. School-Age: Reading Instruction (Grades 1–3)
  5. Primary: Approaches to Children's Writing (Pre-K and K)
  6. School-Age: Writing Opportunities and Instruction (Grades 1–3)
  7. Approaches to Curriculum Integration
  8. Recognizing Diversity in the Classroom

9. Facilitating Home Support for Literacy
10. Approaches to Assessment

These items are scored using a carefully and intentionally designed rubric that ranges from low to high on a 1 to 5 scale:

5 - Exemplary
4 - Proficient
3 - Basic
2 - Limited
1 - Deficient

Observers become familiar with the language of the descriptors of the rubric ratings which are gradients of both quantitative and qualitative differences. Interrater reliability is achieved after sufficient training and practice. Scoring differences between observer pairs should vary by only one point maximum on each of the individual fourteen items.

Observation and preliminary scoring, done during literacy-related instructional time, takes approximately 30–40 minutes. Trained observers schedule the observation with the teacher in advance, making the request to visit during large-group book reading, small group reading instruction, writing activities, and also during learning-center or free-choice times. Observers focus on the teacher, the students, and the environment.

Following the classroom visit and the completion of the *Classroom Observation* section of the toolkit booklet, there is a protocol for the *Teacher Interview*. This 10–15 minute meeting allows observers to query for information about aspects of what was seen that requires further clarification. The scoring should reflect predominantly what was observed, rather than what was reported. Observer training makes this aspect of the tool usage understood in a practical manner. Presence and Use of Technology, as well as some items typically require post-observation questioning of the teacher to clarify or validate information to assist in scoring the items.

After the teacher interview, final scoring of the *Classroom Observation*, based on classroom evidence, is completed. As described in training, and in reviewing the ELLCO documentation, the descriptors of the observable evidence are assigned points of 1, 3, and 5. Observers are encouraged to focus scoring on these points, reserving the scores of 2 and 4 for instances in which there is mixed evidence of the neighboring descriptive scoring points (1, 3, 5). Notations of evidence should be recorded in the area provided for notation. Care is taken during training sessions to highlight the importance of scoring each of the 14 items without bias, referring to the individual rubric criteria for that item; the classroom should not be viewed as a gestalt.

The final component of the ELLCO Toolkit is the *Literacy Activities Rating Scale*. This scale is used following the completion of the *Literacy Environment Checklist* and the *Classroom Observation*. Through the answering of nine questions about book reading and writing, the observer(s) quantify the number of book reading sessions and the number of writing activities by recording observations of the number of books read and the time, in minutes, spent reading, as well as the type and number of writing activities children and adults were engaged in. These activities are noted during the entire classroom visit and the scoring is cumulative. The data is recorded and the scoring yields two subtotal sums—one for book reading and one for written language activities. Looking at these subtotals reveals useful information, though a total summed score is also recorded as the *"Literacy Activities Rating Scale"* score. To provide professional development support or make programmatic suggestions or changes, the reading and writing subscale scores should be looked at individually.

Collation of all collected data from the ELLCO Toolkit is codified on the "Toolkit Score Form" at the end of the ELLCO Toolkit booklet. Transferring all data to these two pages provides a comprehensive and visually manageable snapshot of the total observational landscape. Additionally, having all the data recorded and tabulated on two pages streamlines the use of the collected data for other purposes. Data clerks and researchers can transfer and consolidate data in a manageable manner from this centralized data form to any other storage format.

While the toolkit's three components are designed and intended to be used in synchrony to support systematic observation of early childhood classrooms and practices, the *Classroom Observation and Teacher Interview* alone has been employed by school districts and research projects such as the Connecticut Reading Excellence Act Demonstration Site grant (2002–2004) and Connecticut Reading First grant (2004–2009) to evaluate programs in preschool through grade 3. Users of the ELLCO must make informed decisions regarding its employment based upon individual programmatic needs.

According to the *User's Guide to the Early Language & Literacy Classroom Observation Toolkit, Research Edition* (Smith & Dickinson, 2002), "possibly the most important test for a tool that purports to evaluate the quality of support provided for children's literacy development is the capacity of the tool to predict children's literacy development. The Classroom Observation has been used in correlational research and employed in hierarchical linear modeling designed to determine the contributions of classroom quality to children's receptive vocabulary"(Peabody Picture Vocabulary Test—Third Edition; Dunn and Dunn, 1997) and early literacy scores (Profile of Early Literacy Development; Dickinson & Chaney, 1998, p. 60). The analyses demonstrated that children from low social economic status backgrounds who participated in preschool experiences where they were provided with quality, research-based emergent literacy instruction and opportunities, experience growth in their vocabulary and early literacy skills.

REFERENCES

Begley, S. (1996, February 19). Your child's brain. *Newsweek, 127*(8), 55–61.

Begley, S. (Spring-Summer, 1997). How to build a baby's brain. [Special Issue] *Newsweek, 129*, 28–32.

Bransford, J. D., Brown, A. L. & Cocking, R. (eds) (1999) *How people learn: Brain, mind, experience and school.* Washington DC: National Academy Press.

Bredekamp, S., & Copple, C. (Eds.). (1997). *Developmentally appropriate practice in early childhood programs* (Rev. ed.). Washington, DC: NAEYC.

Burns, S., Griffin, P., & Snow. C. (Eds.). (1999). *Starting out right: A guide to promoting children's reading success.* Washington, DC: National Academy Press. ISBN: 0-309-06410-4

Cadwell, L. B. (1997). *Bringing Reggio Emilia home: An innovative approach to early childhood education.* New York: Teachers College Press.

Carnegie Corporation of New York (1994). *Starting points: Meeting the needs of our youngest children.* Report of the Carnegie task force on meeting the needs of young children. NY: Author.

Curtis, D., & M. Carter. (2003). *Designs for living and learning: Transforming early childhood environments.* St. Paul, MN: Redleaf. Available from NAEYC.

Diamond, Marion C. (1988). *Enriching heredity: The impact of the environment on the anatomy of the brain.* New York: The Free Press.

Diamond, M. C. & J. Hopson. (1998). *Magic trees of the mind.* New York: Dutton Books, Penguin-Putnam Group.

Dombro, C & Trister, D. (1997). *The creative curriculum for infants and toddlers.* Washington, DC: Teaching Strategies, Inc.

Fischer, K. & Rose, S. (1998). Growth cycles of the brain and mind. *Educational Leadership, 56*(3), 56–60

Edwards, C., Gandini, L., & Forman, G. (Eds.). (1993). *The hundred languages of children: The Reggio Emilia approach to early childhood education.* Norwood, NJ: Ablex.

Feeney, S., & Moravcik. E. (1987). A thing of beauty: Aesthetic development in young children. *Young Children, 42*(6), 7-15.

Forman, G. (November, 1993). *How are children's cognitive development affected by the Reggio Emilia approach?* Speech presented at the annual meeting at the National Association for the Education of Young Children, Anaheim, CA.

Gunn, B. K., Simmons, D. C., & Kameenui, E. J. (1995). *Emergent literacy: A synthesis of the research.* [Electronic version]. Eugene, OR: The National Center to Improve the Tools of Educators. Retrieved July 30, 2005 from, http://idea.uoregon.edu:16080/~ncite/documents/techrep/tech19.html

Hart, B, & Risley, T. (1995). *Meaningful differences in the everyday experiences of young American children.* Baltimore: Brookes. ISBN: 1557661979.

Klein, A. S. (2002) Different approaches to teaching: Comparing three preschool programs. [Electronic version]. Retrieved August 1, 2005 from, http://www.earlychildhood.com/Articles/index.cfm?FuseAction=Article&A=367

Lindsey, G. (1999). Brain research and implications for early childhood education. [Electronic version]. *Childhood Education,* Winter 1998/1999. By Stone, Sandra J. Retrieved on August 3, 2005 from, http://www.parentsurf.com/p/articles/mi_qa3614/is_199801/ai_n8807705

Logue, M. (2000). *Implications of brain development research for even start family literacy programs.* Washington, D.C.: U.S. Department of Education.

McCain & Mustard. (1999). *Early years study: Reversing the real brain drain.* Toronto: Government of Ontario. Adapted from Doherty, G. (1997). *Zero to six: The basics for school readiness. Applied research branch.* Ottawa: Human Resources Development Canada.

McNeil, F. (1999). *Brain research and learning—an introduction.* SIN Research Matters No.10. London: Institute of Education.

Morrow, L. M. (1990). Preparing the classroom environment to promote literacy during play. *Early Childhood Research Quarterly, 5,* 537-540.

Murray, B. (2000). From brain scan to lesson plan. *Monitor on Psychology, 31*(3). Retrieved on August 2, 2005 from, http://www.apa.org/monitor/mar00/brainscan.htm

Neuman, S. & Roskos, K. (1993). *Language and literacy learning in the early years: An integrated approach.* Fort Worth, TX: Harcourt Brace Jovanovich.

Neumann, S. B., & Dickinson, D. (Eds.). (2001). *Handbook of early literacy research.* New York: Guilford Press.

Newberger, J. J. (1997). New brain development research-A wonderful window of opportunity to build public support for early childhood education! *Young Children, 52*(4), 4–9.

Shore, R. (1997). *Rethinking the brain: New insights into early development.* NY: Families and Work Institute.

Smith, M., & Dickinson, D. (2002). *User's guide to the early language & literacy classroom observation toolkit, research edition.* Baltimore, Maryland: Paul H. Brookes Publishing Co.

Tarr, P. (2004). Consider the walls. *Young Children, 59*(3), 88–92.

Teale, W. H. & Sulzby, E. (1989). Emergent literacy: New perspectives. In D. S. Strickland & L. M. Morrow (Eds.), *Emerging literacy: Young children learn to read and write* (pp. 1–15). Newark, DE: International Reading Association.

Temple, E., Deutsch, G. K., Poldrack, R. A., Miller, S. L., Tallal, P., Merzenich, M. M. & Gabrieli, J. (2003). Neural deficits in children with dyslexia ameliorated by behavioral remediation: Evidence from functional MRI. *Proceedings of the National Academy of Sciences, 100,* 2860-2865.

Vygotsky, L. (1978). *Mind in society: The development of higher psychological processes.* Cambridge, MA: Harvard University Press.

White House Archive. (1999): *"How are the children?" Report on early childhood development and learning.* [Electronic version]. Retrieved on July 23, 2005, from http://www.ed.gov/pubs/How_Children/foreword.html

Simmons, T. & Sheehan, R. (1997, February 16). Brain research manifests importance of first years. [Electronic version]. *The News & Observer.* Retrieved from, http://www.nando.net/nao/2little2late/ stories/day1-main.html p. 26 (http://www.whitehouse.gov/firstlady/initiatives/education/earlychildhood.htm)

Chapter Three

Developmental Supervision: Case Studies

Maureen Ruby

"Developmental supervision" is a form of supervision intended to provide support and mentoring to teachers in a spirit of collaboration and promotion of individual and system-wide professional development. As described in the Literacy Environment Enrichment Program (LEEP), there are several key elements involved in "developmental supervision":

- Supervision is a system rather than an isolated event
- Supervision occurs on an ongoing and regular basis for all staff
- Supervision is a supportive, collaborative process
- Supervision is a skill which requires training and support to master

In thinking about supervision in this way, "supervision" is a positive experience for all involved and, in fact, is the "lifeblood" of the early childhood education program. This is in stark contrast to the archetype in which supervision is viewed as punitive, a "necessary evil" or an "event" triggered by error or inferior performance on the part of the supervisee. When supervision is viewed in this way, or as a required "component" of the annual evaluation and paperwork mandates, it serves little positive purpose in ongoing development of quality professionals and early childhood educational opportunities for children.

In the world of the developing professional, quality, ongoing support, and supervision is viewed as a "right" and all employees, even the more experienced and "seasoned" teachers, are entitled to opportunities to reflect with a supervisor on their needs in dealing with challenges, as well as to share their successes and effective strategies. In essence, supervision is a vital component of professional development, which should embrace each and every staff member. As a collaborative process, excellent and open communication is both crucial and fundamental. Together, supervisors and supervisees are invested in the setting of agendas, expectations, and coming to a joint understanding of job expectations, responsibilities and performance criteria. In such a format of collaboration, there is a mutual understanding of a shared responsibility to reflect upon what is observed by a supervisor, as well as the need to dedicate time for analysis of current classroom practices and the alignment thereof with "best practices." The "team" can then develop and document an action plan, which serves both as a blueprint for future collaboration and a springboard for planning professional development. With established guidelines and routines for communication, a professional relationship can be cultivated that further supports goal attainment for the good of the professional staff and, most importantly, translates into an all-around enhanced educational experience for the children entrusted to the teachers.

Teachers who are treated with respect and as professionals, gain not only knowledge, but also an increased level of self-esteem. This can foster a confidence and a desire to seek advanced training and enrollment in educational programs that leads to post secondary and graduate level degrees in early childhood education. Building knowledge in course content in child development and behavior, as well as in early literacy and content areas such as science, will enhance the experiences of both children and adults. When supervisors are learning side-by-side with teachers through pre-observational conferencing, observation, analytical reflection, and planning, they are better able to "see the whole picture," to be invested in the day-to-day workings of the classrooms, to connect with the students' experiences, and ultimately are better prepared to support the teachers. Developmental supervision, as a process, serves as a model for future early childhood supervisors. Teachers tend to "teach the way they were taught," and excellence in supervision can lead to excellent future supervisors and a strengthening of the field.

Caruso and Fawcett (1999) list and describe eight myths about supervision. They state that the etiology of these myths is tied to a variety of issues including supervisors' personal, individual expectations concerning their own supervisory experiences, training and education; the attitudes that staff members have about supervisors; and their personal job expectations. Some of these beliefs and internal stressors are true, others are totally erroneous, while others may have some partial truth implanted. Myths identified by Caruso and Fawcett (p. 3) include:

- Almost anyone can be an early childhood supervisor
- There is one best supervisory approach to take with everyone
- Supervisors have all the answers

- Direct confrontation with staff is non-supportive
- Skilled supervisors never engage in manipulation
- Good teachers do not need supervision
- Supervision is an objective process
- Supervisors are always calm

Caruso and Fawcett "emphasize the dynamic relationship between supervisor and supervisee" (p. 46) in their attempt to "underscore that staff members are not the object of supervision, but play an active role in the process, and that the supervisors learn, change, and grow as a result of the process too." (p. 46) They stress that supervision is a "caring process." Both supervisors and teachers give and receive "care"—care is reciprocal. Caregivers, they state, lose their drive when their care is unrequited. Positive response to care is a motivator to the caregiver and fuels the cycle of caring. Temple and Fawcet refer to the work of Nel Noddings, who in 1992 described four essential components of the ethics of "care." She cites these as being *modeling, dialogue, practice, and confirmation*. Caring supervisors are in essence modeling caring behavior for teachers. She states, ". . . the capacity to care may be dependent on having adequate experience in being cared for." (Caruso & Temple, 1999, p5). Dialogue supports critical thinking in that people who are connected and relating to each other in communicative relationships, will likely discuss and explore ideas with each other prior to making decisions. Without open dialogue within relationships, there is little sharing of ideas and information and no opportunity for learning from each other. When teachers and students "practice" caring in the school environment, there is the likelihood that this practice will become internalized and eventually transcend the school environment. Thus the caring behavior will be enacted in the world beyond the schoolhouse. When supervisors are employing the concepts and principles of "developmental supervision," they will be involved in more positive than punitive actions with supervisees. This will result in greater opportunities to engage in affirming rather than criticizing interactions. By confirming teachers' positive practices, supervisors are motivating the teachers to not only continue to do their jobs as best as they can, but also they are modeling behaviors of affirming and valuing the actions and contributions of the children.

Clearly, observation is a key element in the role of any supervisor. It is from observation that supervisors can directly experience the work of a teacher and begin to determine and design effective individual support. During an observational experience, a supervisor must collect data. The data collection documents what has been observed, serves as a basis for reflection and conferencing, and establishes a record for measuring growth and progress. In this light, an observation is far from "negative" or "punitive" in nature. Clinical developmental supervision entails much more than a scheduled observation of a teacher in his/her classroom practice. Rather, much care and planning goes into making the actual observation a *part* of an ongoing cycle (Caruso, 1999, pp.103–149). The cycle consists of the following stages:

- Pre-observation conference
- Observation
- Analysis and strategy
- Supervision conference
- Post-conference analysis

Pre-Observation Conference time supports the development of effective, positive working relationships; establishing trust; open lines of communication; set goals; establish routines; schedule observations, and define objectives. The pre-observation conference provides an opportunity for teachers to freely ask questions and share concerns.

Observation takes place during a pre-agreed upon time in which the teacher and supervisor agreed upon the type of observation and the tools that would be used. Plans made during the pre-observation conference are observed in practice. The supervisor should be attentive to the questions raised by the teacher in the pre-observation conference while the actual observation is taking place.

Analysis and Strategy involves the supervisor taking the time to analyze the data collected during the observation in light of the pre-observational discussion and questions. The supervisor reflects patterns of behavior, incidents observed, and takes the opportunity to process how to best facilitate the teacher in reflecting about her practice during the supervisory conference. While a teacher may desire immediate feedback following the observation, it is also important for the teacher to reflect and think before the conference.

Supervisory Conference time is a time for teachers to share reflections about their own analysis of the observed lesson and for the supervisor to support the teacher's reflection and analysis and provide feedback. Together, the team can plan strategies to deal with areas of concern. The positive aspects of the observation are highlighted. Reflection upon the observational data is used to inform future instructional plans and to plan for professional development opportunities. When teachers reflect, they can make connections between their practice and teaching strategies and students' observed behaviors. In this way, self assessment will inform future instructional practice. Active listening is a critical skill for supervisors during this period. Simple questions that encourage thinking and reflection, as well as questions that promote consideration of alternate decisions and predictions help teachers plan for future lessons.

Post-conference Analysis is a period of individual reflection by both the teacher and the supervisor. During this time, both self assess their communication, strategies, roles and effectiveness during the supervisory conference. The supervisor thinks about how effective she was in working with the teacher and what next steps she can take to support the teacher's professional development.

The cycle of clinical developmental supervision is a win-win-win situation. Teachers grow through the direct support of the supervisor, as well as through the development of self-reflective skills. Supervisors improve their observational and reflective skills, which often lead to further professional development planning for both themselves and for their teachers. Students are the ultimate winners in the equation where supervisors and teachers engage in active developmental supervision practices. Learning environments in which adults are collaborating to improve practice via reflection and professional development are environments that are able to respond to the observed needs of children on a regular basis.

DEVELOPMENTAL SUPERVISION IN LEEP

Developmental Supervision infused into the LEEP Curriculum strives to create learning environments that enhance children's early language and literacy learning. The unique opportunity to have teacher-supervisor teams learn side-by-side in both the didactic/coursework component and in the practicum/classroom component with on-site faculty support and consultation is the basis of the success of the curriculum. Success is not limited to novice teachers, and new supervisors. In reviewing case studies of teacher-supervisor teams from LEEP, it is clear that all teachers and supervisors can benefit in documented ways from this methodology including the most experienced teachers and supervisors and novice teams. What's more, all students can be successful in their learning with appropriate instruction guided by "developmental supervision."

A CASE STUDY: PRESCHOOL CLASSROOM WITH A LEEP SUPERVISOR: SUPERVISEE TEAM

A Public School Pre School Setting

A case that clearly evidences the power of developmental supervision in early literacy learning is one from a special needs preschool class in an urban priority school district. Both the teacher and the supervisor were enrolled in the

Literacy Environment Enrichment Program class. The approach to the developmental supervision learning experience was framed within the perspective of the district's approach to fulfilling their commitments to inclusive education, balanced literacy, embedded professional development, and compliance with local, state, and federal education mandates.

The children in the preschool class all have significant developmental delays. Each of the children receives speech and language services as well as occupational therapy weekly. There are no typical peers in this classroom, although the students have opportunities with students from neighboring classes. As described by their teacher, Laura, her students' language abilities range from what Weitzman and Greenberg describe as Stage 2, Communicator to Stage 5, Early Sentence User, (Weitzman & Greenberg, 2002, p. 41–49).

"Typically developing children are Communicators from about eight to thirteen months . . . An older child with a language delay may be a Communicator. Children who are language delayed and who stay at the Communicator stage longer . . . have difficulty using words" (Weitzman, E. & Greenberg, J. 2002, p.4.).Weitzman and Greenberg explain that these language-delayed Communicators attempt to communicate with gestures, facial expressions and sounds. It is important that a teacher recognize that the limited expressive language ability does not necessarily mean that there is a similar receptive impairment. It is possible that for many of these children, they have an ability to comprehend language that is much advanced from their expressive language development. Though they may not have a concrete and clear understanding of words, despite an appearance that they do, they can be most successful with mediated scaffolding through explicit cueing, which might include actions, tone, gesturing, and being familiar with situations.

Typically developing early sentence users are two to three years of age and use sentences of two-to-five words in brief conversational exchanges. When language delayed children are in this stage, they often have not internalized the rules of grammar, verb agreement, pronoun usage, tense, conversational turn-taking—which may also be limited by comprehension. Typically, early sentence users will repeatedly inquire, "why?" They start to tell loosely woven, hard to follow narratives; try to communicate feelings; and may begin to use language to express imagination.

REFLECTIONS ON THE LEEP EXPERIENCE

In the beginning of the LEEP program, Grace, an educator of twenty plus years with advanced degrees in literacy and supervision, described her "pre-LEEP" supervisory role.

My experience with supervision has been to use a narrative limited to a particular focus. This focus usually consists of observing an explicit small group for the before, during, and after a literacy activity or the management and content of individual literacy practices. I script to the specific purpose, seldom using a checklist. I do use the conference components of pre-conference, observation, analysis and post-conference. One area which I have neglected is post-conference analysis. From my experiences with Laura, I realize how important it is to take the time to reflect on the strategies used during the conference, my role, as well as the role of the staff member. This reflection will promote my own growth as a supervisor, which in turn will promote growth within the staff.

Grace indicated that she was influenced after the initial LEEP sessions to reflect on how she interacts with teachers. The assignments included videotaping in the classroom during literacy activities as well as videotaping conferencing between the teacher and the supervisee. She said that she would prioritize visiting classrooms more often.

It takes frequent visits in order synthesize the dynamics of the make up of the classroom, understand the professional strengths and needs of the teacher, and develop a rapport with the teacher and students. Immersion in the environment is necessary for effective conferencing to occur. Secondly, I have a new awareness of the power of filming as a learning tool. Being able to replay the observation and the conference expanded the depth of reflection and analysis far beyond what could have seen and synthesized from an observation script. Finally, the supervisor determines the effectiveness of the conference as a learning tool for staff by being sensitive to the types of questions asked. The right questions will determine if conference goals are met and encourage the supervisee to analyze his/her own behavior. The right questions lead the supervisee to self discovery.

ORAL LANGUAGE DEVELOPMENT

Though dealing with a very challenging situation, Laura and her supervisor, Grace, discussed the importance of providing opportunities for communication to children from birth. In these activities the adult does most of the communicating, but it is here that the foundation is laid for the child's ability to communicate in conversations. From birth, children need to hear their caregivers talk. Infants, as well as older, language delayed children must be treated as turn takers. Cognizant of this, Laura employs this principle of talking to a child as if he/she can talk to you. Only one of her students began the year engaging in verbal conversation, and even his responses are one or two words. Laura recognized the need to ask lots of questions. To support joint interaction, Laura often turns her conversation to the child's interest. To do so, activities which involve turn taking are incorporated into daily routines during circle time. Laura regularly joins the children in play activities, and as a result, the children use more language in response to her questions.

Most of Laura's students started the year communicating via use of one word; a few were just beginning to combine words. One student, Alice has remained at the communicator stage, although her ability to understand language is much more advanced than her ability to express herself in language. A boy named James is the only student using 4 or 5 word sentences. He would respond to a question once, but he would not engage in an ongoing conversation Another child speaks only when she needs or wants to do something. She, however, readily engages in creative play. Through play interactions, Laura sees the opportunity to develop language. Laura recognized after observation and reflection that though her students were not progressing naturally from nonverbal to verbal communication, they did have the physical ability to say the words. She attempted to "manipulate" snack time to promote language. She encourages language by having children ask for their needs to be fulfilled. What was clear to Laura, her supervisor and her LEEP instructor was the fact that her students all needed an enormous amount of scaffolded language experience to facilitate their use of language.

Grace noted that in Chapter 3 of Weitzman and Greenberg the statement was made that "Children who lead get the language they need." She felt an important message was that teachers must put into practice in their classrooms strategies that permit children to take the lead. This would allow for teaching to center around the child. Children could then choose what they wish to say and build on their own interests. In this type of environment language can flourish. In her written reflections, Grace said, "Teachers can let go of the lead by not being so concerned with getting the child to talk. Instead, environments need to be created that encourage children to talk because they want to talk." Weitzman & Greenberg write; ". . . the motivating force for communication comes from within, from the desire to connect with others and feel the satisfaction that results from that connection." (Weitzman & Greenberg, 2002. p. 5) The first author observed this strategy in action in Laura's class when she played with the children at center time, making herself part of the activity that interests them.

Alice, a student who is hesitant to talk, will talk only to Laura during classroom interactions. Grace described trying to "make" Anna talk to her, without spending time interacting with her in center time. This was unsuccessful. She realized the need to develop a rapport with Alice and encourage her by developing a purpose for engaging in a conversation with her. Grace observed, "Letting the child take the lead requires observing, waiting, and listening. Observe to see what interests a child or what he/she is trying to say. Wait to give a child time to initiate or get involved in an activity of his/her choice. Listen so that you really hear what the child is saying and can respond appropriately. This is active listening. It would not be a bad idea to practice active listening in all life situations. Imagine how relationships would change!" She observed that interactions with children must be on their level, being physically face to face with them, in contrast to the usual stance of looking down at them. "At this time you may even join in playing with a child in a center. Follow a child's lead by becoming interested in their interests. Imitating what a child says can also be a motivator for very young children." Grace and Laura discovered that this technique was effective with the language delayed children in Laura's room. When a child is at a loss for language, the teacher can also support the child by putting into words what he/she knows the child wants to say. This is validating as it lets the child know that she is understood. What began to happen when Laura conspicuously employed strategies such as these in her classroom was that the children began to engage in more deliberate and active responding. It was encouraging and motivating to think that as the year continued, the responses would become more frequent and would begin to resemble and to emerge into bonafide conversations.

PHONOLOGICAL AWARENESS

Phonological awareness is the ability to hear the similarities and differences in the sounds of words. In LEEP teachers and supervisors learn that phonological awareness is an overarching term, like an umbrella, that encompasses all sound segments in a speech stream—including words; syllables; rhymes; initial, medial, and final sounds; and phonemes. Phonemes are the smallest units of speech sounds. When children become aware of these differences they can begin to understand how to play with sounds in spoken language by making up rhymes and interacting with words in nursery rhymes, poems, conversation, and songs. Phonemic Awareness (PA) is the ability to manipulate the sounds heard in spoken words and the understanding that spoken words and syllables are made up of sequences of speech sounds (Yopp, 1992).

These skills with manipulating sounds are essential to learning to read in the alphabetic writing system of English, Spanish, and other languages, because in alphabetic languages letters represent sounds or phonemes. Without phonemic awareness, later phonics instruction will make little sense. Without appropriate language experience and opportunity to develop phonological and ultimately phonemic awareness, a child may not be able to assess that "mom" and "monkey" begin with the same sound or may not be able to blend the sounds /zzzzzzziiiiiiiipppppppppp/ into the word "zip". When the time comes to associate sounds with written symbols (letters) to enable the child to write the symbols that match the sounds heard in words, and thus transcribe sound to speech, a child will be at a great loss without phonemic awareness skills. "One of the most compelling and well-established findings in the research on beginning reading is the important relationship between phonemic awareness and reading acquisition." (Kame'enui, et. al., 1997, p.7).

In LEEP, teachers and supervisors engage in detailed didactic sessions, including video clips, as well as participate in small and large group activities to experiment with phonemic awareness games that children enjoy. Group discussion and reflection clarifies and reviews the concepts for participants. Teachers are required to complete a series of phonological awareness activities as a follow-up assignment to their in class session. These activities are carried out over several weeks and include activities demonstrated in LEEP, activities from a variety of independent sources, or activities developed by the teacher. Supervisors observe a phonological awareness activity and videotape the observed lesson. Following the lesson, the supervisory conference is videotaped. At a subsequent date, both videos are viewed by the supervisor and supervisee with a LEEP faculty member.

During Grace's observation of a phonological awareness activity, she noted that "Laura engaged the students in a playful activity with the goal of having children clap the sounds in their names. The names were on cards with the syllables color coded and cut apart. Laura would flip the card as the child's name was spoken. Each child was addressed individually by Laura singing this song, "Your name is Alice, Alice, Alice. Your name is Alice. What's your name?" The children's attention was better when music was part of the learning. Laura would say the name, flip the card, then say the name again while clapping. The children would then clap their name. Anna, James and Charlie were able to clap the number of parts in their name. Charlie also clapped and spoke all the children's names and as he did, one could observe the smile of satisfaction on his face. He was the new child in the classroom that day. This activity allowed him to feel good about himself and his environment. I could not help but think that the feeling of achievement he displayed during this experience would positively impact his learning in this class. The children did not make use of the name cards, as recognizing their name in print was not developmentally appropriate. Throughout the activity Laura continued to offer positive feedback with words such as, "Good job Charlie!," "Help me!," and "You try it". Laura expressed that she will continue to engage the children in a variety of interactive activities to hear the parts of words."

SUPERVISOR'S REFLECTION ON PHONOLOGICAL AWARENESS ACTIVITY

Prior to the conference, Grace had visited Laura's room not only for the observation, but on many other occasions. She had learned it was important to the success of developmental supervision for her to be familiar with the classroom, Laura's teaching style, as well as the strengths and weaknesses of the students. These frequent visits helped to establish a positive working relationship between supervisor and supervisee. The children also became comfortable with Grace as a visitor to their classroom and they actually welcomed her. Laura and Grace met briefly a few days before each observation to establish the goals for the lesson, and so that Grace would be familiar with the strategies and materials Laura would be using.

At each conference, Grace began by restating the goals and strategies brought forth by Laura during the pre-conference. Laura had the opportunity to verbalize the accuracy of this information, which reinforced what had been agreed upon and also the fact that Grace was attentive and invested in the relationship. Grace next asked, "With these goals in mind, what do you think about the activities I observed?" This question was designed to allow Laura to reflect out loud on the activities in relation to the goals that Grace had just summarized. Laura felt there was some success in achieving her goals and also reflected on the individual factors that contributed to differences in student outcomes and responses. These factors included use of reflective and expressive language, distractibility, ability to focus, neurological disorders, and the arrival of Charlie as a new student to the classroom. Grace encouraged Laura to think deeper by asking, "Was the goal met in terms of your expectation for engagement by the students?" Laura stated that she felt the goal was high in relation to all the activity in the room. This question elicited talking about her own reflection and changes she had already made in her literacy environment since the observations. She had taken down some of the visuals, which she felt were over stimulating. Having noticed that the children respond positively to music, she had made circle time song-based with a particular sequence so the children learned the routine and knew what was coming next. This need for structure had become obvious as she began to teach in a more explicit and goal oriented manner. Laura also realized the need to engage the children kinesthetically, so she added physical movement to the activities. She was cognizant of the fact that the amount of movement each child can deal with effectively is very different. She also realized that it was critical to consider the individual needs and abilities of each child as she planned activities.

In the next part of the conference, Grace addressed two observations that had not been previously touched on. First, she observed that at one point during the activity James had to be removed from the group. She wondered if something could have been done to avoid James' removal. Laura responded that this is what works for James when he becomes over stimulated. He did return to the circle shortly after he was removed and was able to participate appropriately. It became clear to Grace that Laura's understanding of James' needs turned what appeared to be somewhat negative and exclusionary to the supervisor, into a positive for James. This highlighted the importance of open communication and its key role in developmental supervision. Grace also addressed the manner in which Laura expanded upon the one-word answers from the children to provide a good model of language. Laura displayed caring for the students through her verbal praise and encouragement via expressions such as "Good Job" and "I like the way you are looking at the books."

A strength of these conference sessions was that they ended with planning for "next steps." Laura had already spoken about using more music based activities which have a calming, focusing affect on her children. She planned to provide the children with an abundance and variety of opportunities to listen and respond to the parts in their names with movement. After discussion and reflection with Grace and the LEEP faculty member, she decided not to use the children's name cards in phonological awareness activities as they are not developmentally appropriate. Phonological awareness concerns itself with "sound" not with "print." Grace made plans to visit the classroom the following week.

Grace's stated goal for the conference was for Laura to think reflectively about teaching and learning in her classroom in relation to phonological awareness. During the sessions Laura was reflective in looking at the appropriateness of the materials and strategies used in relationship to her children's development. Grace attributed a big part of the effectiveness of the conference to Laura's self reflective nature. From the reflective conferencing, after viewing and discussing the videotape, Laura decided she would no longer use the name cards and would continue to provide playful activities to help children distinguish sounds in words. Additionally, she had already reflected and made changes in the room. These changes included songs in center time, more opportunities for children to become physically engaged, and enlarging the play area. The sessions also established a positive conference climate where supervisor and supervisee work together. Grace wrote, "I readily admitted to Laura that I did not have all the answers, as her evidence changed my perception of removing James from the group."

She went on to say, "From this experience I learned that being a supervisor is not an easy task. Conducting an effective, reflective conference takes planning and practice in order to ask the right questions at the right time. Questions must be used strategically to encourage reflection and growth on the part of both the supervisee and the supervisor. The supervisor has the responsibility to provide the support the supervisee needs to reflect on teaching and learning. The supervisee is entitled to objective feedback, assistance in improving their skills, assistance in assessing the effectiveness of their program, and guidance in practicing developmentally appropriate strategies in their classrooms. It takes practice on the part of the supervisor to make this happen."

Grace learned, through viewing the supervisory conference video, that during the conferences she offered information too quickly. "There were times if I had remained quiet I am sure Laura would have continued to reflect on her own. It was difficult for me not to add my 'two cents.' Effective listening is a skill I need to practice." Had she not had the opportunity to engage in a post observation supervisory conference and had the benefit of viewing the conference, she would not have gained this insight and been able to grow professionally.

Grace determined that there was a need to end the conference with more specific plans for next actions. Watching the tapes, she evaluated the goals for the next steps and determined that they were vague. She commented that she should have said, "Lets brainstorm together to plan some specific next steps."

This example demonstrates that the developmental supervision process promotes collaboration with a focus on teaching, learning, and reflection. When educators take the time for reflection, there's a much needed opportunity to *think about* whether or not what we are doing in our classrooms is good for children and is supporting their developing literacy needs. All stakeholders have responsibility in the process, but the supervisor must take the lead in making the process work.

EMERGENT WRITING

Writing does not begin with formal penmanship instruction! Children go through a variety of developmental stages of writing before they arrive on the kindergarten doorstep. It begins with scribbling and drawing, progresses to a letter-like formation stage, and is further refined as children actually form letters, display directionality and linearity, and map speech onto generated print. Teachers spend time learning to create a learning environment that promotes and develops opportunities for young children to see writing modeled, to be exposed to and to understand a variety of purposes for writing, and to take risks and experiment with written language. Teachers and supervisors together analyze children's written language samples and reflect on the individual children's stages of writing development. Concurrently, teams are using this analysis to reflect on what types of opportunities and scaffolds different students need to continue successfully on their developmental path in writing.

Following LEEP lessons and activities on emergent writing, Laura incorporated new experiences focusing on written language activities into her classroom. These activities provided children with developmentally appropriate and engaging opportunities to experiment with writing. Children were provided with direct access to a wide variety of writing implements including varying sizes, shapes, colors and textures of paper, clipboards, materials to make signs, Wikki Sticks, white boards with markers, pencils, crayons, colored chalk, and foam paint. These materials were not limited to an "art" area, but were distributed throughout each of the centers in the classroom environment. A special writing center was established to showcase writing and to distinguish it from "art" and other activities. This presentation gave writing the respect of a place all its own while incorporating this communication form into all areas of the literacy environment. Laura provided the children with an engaging activity that involved fine motor skill practice, hand-eye coordination practice and the formation of letters. After explanation and modeling, the children were observed making letters on the white board with Wikki Sticks. Laura first demonstrated this activity by making the letter T. Each child was given an opportunity to make the letter T, while Laura offered guidance when needed. All children were eager to interact with this new medium. Alice put the first line of the T on the board. Ever mindful of language development, Laura used this opportunity to encourage language pointing out the "top" of the white board and the "top" of the letter. She cued Alice to say "top" before she added the other line. Alice was so eager to use the Wikki Sticks that she did not exhibit her usual reluctance to speak. Later, during center time, Alice again chose to make lines with the Wikki Sticks. Spontaneously and independently, Alice began to use a marker to put writing between each line. Laura talked with Alice about the pattern she had created of lines and writing, taking time to expand the understanding of the task Alice had completed. Seeing the flurry of activity and excitement around Alice, two other students, who are usually reluctant participants, were also eager to take their turn at using the Wikki Sticks. By offering this new experience, Laura had engaged all the children, which is critical for promoting learning.

Laura provided materials to make signs for use in interactive play in the cars and trucks area. She put a collection of red and green paper, popsicle sticks, and markers in a container and placed it in the center. She facilitated this activity by asking James, Charlie and Alice, individually, if they would like to make a sign. The children were given "free choice" to decide if they wanted to be part of this activity. James and Alice were happy to participate in the sign making. Using a book on "neighborhoods" Laura pointed out the traffic signs on the pages. She then modeled the use of the materials and explained what she was doing as she created a sign. Laura engaged the children by questioning and showing, not merely telling. James made a stop sign and then proceeded to use it in interactive play. Alice made a go sign. Laura stayed with the children, observing and engaging in questioning, and continued to support the activity as needed. When the signs were complete, the children began to say the words themselves as they played with the signs. Laura reinforced the children's learning by staying somewhat parallel, yet intermittently modeling the meaning that the signs conveyed as the children used them in their continuing play.

Laura added writing materials to her science center. Alice was particularly intrigued with using the clipboard. When observed looking at objects under the microscope, Laura approached and asked her if she would like to write about what she was seeing. Understanding, Alice immediately picked up the clipboard and began to write. Laura began to dictate descriptions of the objects. Anna would repeat some of Laura's words. When Laura said the acorn got bigger, Alice said "Big!" and wrote on her clipboard paper. When Alice appeared to be finished writing, Laura said, "Don't forget your name." Alice immediately wrote more on the paper. It was clear that Alice was largely understanding the meaning of the words and the experience. Laura was successful in using the strategy of "interrupting" for Alice and by supplying language she brought meaning to Alice's message.

All the children were observed participating in a gross motor activity, painting with foam paint. Laura's intent was to offer practice with crossing the midline, a skill needed in writing. The children enjoyed the activity as evidenced in their requests for more paint. This was an activity that provided an opportunity for everyone to participate and complete the activity with a high level of success. It is clear that children must come to an understanding that print contains a message. Laura's children did come to appreciate this despite the fact that the stages of emergent writing in this class range from unrelated scribble to some repetitive marks.

The infusion of a variety of emergent writing materials into the literacy environment fostered an enthusiasm among the children for experimenting with writing activities. Every student wanted a turn using the Wikki Sticks. The carry-over of this enthusiasm supported sustained motivation in the writing center, where the children continued to make shapes with the Wikki Sticks. Alice used the clipboard in both the science and cars and trucks centers. When Alice would begin to "write" Laura expanded upon her learning by verbalizing what she surmised Alice wanted to say. As Alice's expressive language is so delayed, Laura scaffolded Alice's learning by trying to supply her with language and labels for what she appeared to be thinking. Through this activity and the accompanying teacher support, Alice was provided with carefully designed and planned opportunities to be motivated to talk. Three students, who were motivated almost daily to play with the cars and trucks, had the opportunity to build upon their interest and comfort level and to expand their learning by making and using signs in their play. Laura skillfully introduced and integrated this activity during engaging play and almost seamlessly, the students were motivated to make signs and to use them in their imaginative play. Appropriately, the children's own interest was used as the springboard to segue into writing. In the words of Schickedanz (1999) "In the beginning stages, writing and other aspects of literacy are nurtured when children are given opportunities to explore and discover." (p. 2) By providing a variety of writing materials throughout the early childhood literacy environment, children are able to engage in many nurturing writing and literacy opportunities that are a natural outgrowth of familiar and comfortable activities.

BOOK PLANNING AND READING

LEEP dedicates a concentrated effort to support teachers and supervisors in their understanding of the various aspects of book reading in the preschool early literacy environment. Participants gain experience in understanding genres and assessing the types of books available in their classrooms; in understanding strategies for reading books in ways that engage and inform children by planning for before, during, and after reading activities; and in understanding how to integrate books in the classroom to support the curriculum, children's language, and knowledge development while creating a literacy-rich environment.

Teachers assignments included inventorying their classroom book collections, including logging title, author, genre, and a brief description of the content; conducting a "concepts About Print" assessment with a focus child; and creating and implementing book reading planning guides. Supervisors were required to conduct and videotape an observation and supervisory conference.

Laura used her book as a springboard for a variety of learning activities throughout her classroom environment. Her intended focus for this lesson was the journey of a mailed letter. Now that the children had a rich interest in writing, she wanted the children to follow the path of a letter from the postbox to the mailbox. Through this book-supported unit, the children would understand the vocabulary associated with the journey of a letter. Words would include: mail, letter, pouch, postman, and mailbox. Her goal included that children would be able to describe the path of a letter and the role of the postman. She expected variation in children's responses based on individual differences. She felt she could assess their varying levels of cognitive understanding by their responses. James, who has a higher level of command of expressive language spoke about the path of a letter as he said, "Send it to grandma." He opened his letter and stated he wanted to add, "P.S. Love Grandma" demonstrating his clear understanding that a letter contains a message. He was able to link the concept of mail to his personal life outside the classroom. When entering the post office center, Alice immediately began to write a letter. Next she playfully "bought" a stamp, put it on her letter, and sealed it. Jonathan nodded yes when asked if he wanted to write a letter. He enjoyed dressing up as the mailman and carrying the mail pouch. James and Charles drove around in the makeshift mail truck. As children have a much higher level of receptive language than expressive language, their knowledge and understanding is assessed by their actions rather than words.

Laura planned for this lesson by choosing the book, *Whose Got Mail*. This book is an early emergent level text with plenty of picture clues and boxes on each page with moveable "flaps." The level was developmentally appropriate for her students. She effectively employed the READ process during the lesson. READ is an acronym for: Read with expression, Expect attention, Adjust, and Discuss. Laura's varied voice level and expression kept the children focused during the reading. She kept their attention through effective questioning. James got up at one point during the read aloud to look closer at the cover of the book. Laura gave him an opportunity to look and responded, "That's something special. You are going to have a turn." James' curiosity was satisfied and he sat back down. The children were attentive and eager to manipulate the flaps on the boxes, and they caught on to the pattern and began to anticipate what would be behind each flap. James, who has more developed expressive language skills than his peers, called out, "Mail, it's a letter, and it's a cat." The other children's responses were relayed by their excited facial expression and gesturing. While reading, Laura adjusted for the children's needs. She varied her voice level and rate, refocused a child by touch while reading, and explicitly talked to James when he became overly excited. She was able to sign "Stop!" without interrupting her flow too much. Laura kept the lesson discussion focused on the goals she had planned.

Laura's questioning strategies encouraged the children to think and supported their oral language. She provided sentence starters after she questioned. She connected questions to personal experience by asking "Who gets the mail at your house?" and "Have you ever gotten a letter?" From the very beginning she raised the children's curiosity level by asking children to predict as she displayed the cover of the book and asked, "What do you think we are going to read about today?" James responded, "A letter." Next Laura asked "What's mail?," James blurted, "People." Laura made a connection for James and responded, "That's right, James, people mail letters." Throughout the lesson, Laura continued using this strategy, continuously connecting for students, and supporting and assessing their understanding.

Grace visited Laura's classroom when the children were involved in creative play in their classroom post office. Laura engaged the children by asking questions and following up on their responses. She had asked James if there was any mail for her today. He said yes and went and got her some envelopes. When he brought the envelopes to her she said "I love getting mail. Do you have any more for me?" James responded, "Yes, but you don't need more." Laura responded, "I guess your right. I have enough for today." Laura's cueing and prompting helped James expand his oral language and engage in conversational turn-taking. Grace observed clinical evidence of growth in language use. Some children, who would only use gestural responses a few short months ago, were now responding to questions with one and two word responses. James had advanced to using four or five word sentences and asking his own questions. Laura was also aware of this and regularly planned activities during circle time and throughout the day which incorporated turn taking.

TEACHER–SUPERVISOR CONFERENCE REFLECTION: BOOK READING

Grace began the conference by reviewing Laura's goals for the observation. This strategy was beneficial in focusing supervisor and supervisee as to the purpose of the lesson. Laura reiterated that her focus for reading *Whose Got Mail* was to help children learn about the journey that a letter takes from post box to mailbox. Additionally, she had a vocabulary focus and wanted to teach the children about the concepts of mail, mailbox, pouch, letter, and postman. Thinking about the lesson, Grace asked, "Do you think your goals for the children's engagement and learning were met?" The question was designed to help Laura first reflect on the outcome of the lesson. Laura felt that James, who functions at a higher cognitive level than the other children, had achieved all the goals of the lesson. She based her response on her assessment of his oral responses. Laura shared her observations of the other children. By their play activities with the props in housekeeping area—turned "post office" she felt the children's play behavior attested to their comprehension.

Grace was responsive to Laura's comment and assessment of the children's demonstration of their learning. She reiterated that there is a wide range of ability levels coexisting in Laura's classroom. Grace next asked, "What are some of the things you did to promote the students' comprehension?" She was attempting to encourage Laura to reflect more deeply about the strategies she used to promote learning for this group of children. Laura detailed what she had selected to use and why. She chose a flip book to hold the students' attention, selected a few vocabulary words with accompanying props, connected background knowledge from their own experiences to the book and subject, and she used picture clues throughout the reading and picture cards at the end of the lesson to summarize. They next had a discussion about the follow up activity in housekeeping/post office, in which the children could freely explore and interact with the props. It was clear to Grace that Laura was strategic in her planning. She knew that the children's attention would be captured by putting all new gel pens, note cards, colored paper, and stickers for stamps in the writing box. By using a variety of questions and motivating comments in the follow up activity, Laura felt she promoted engagement and conversations. In reflecting about these conversations, Laura commented that it is extremely challenging to engage the students in peer-to-peer conversations. In thinking and looking at the video clips, it became clear that she does all the modeling and questioning herself. Acknowledging this led to brainstorming and planning for next steps. It was decided to try to invite typical peers from a neighboring class to join Laura's class for a future book reading and follow up activity. Grace agreed to meet with Laura after this book reading to discuss and compare what happened that might be different.

Grace's goal was to support Laura's deeper reflection regarding her role in helping the students develop oral language to a greater extent. Laura had set this goal for herself. By viewing the video, Laura was better able to observe and reflect upon her children's limitations in using oral language. It was clear that peer-to-peer conversations are limited in Laura's classroom. Laura came up with the idea of inviting other peers to a planned book reading to encourage more peer conversations. Grace had thought of suggesting this herself, but instead supported Laura's own thinking about her classroom practice and her students' needs. Having thought of this on her own, Laura is eager to incorporate this strategy into her next book read.

After this third conference, Grace wrote, "I feel I did a better job of allowing Laura to reflect, before adding my own observations. This was a definite weakness of mine in the previous conferences. I accomplished this by asking more astute questions for the purpose of extending Laura's reflection to a deeper level. 'What else did you do to promote comprehension, and what other strategies did you employ to encourage the children's use of language?'

These two questions allowed Laura more reflection time. I reiterate that being a supervisor is not an easy task! Conducting an effective conference takes planning on the part of the supervisor! Questions must be used strategically to encourage reflection and growth on the part of the supervisee. The supervisor must take the lead and initiative to make this process work."

The case study of Grace and Laura demonstrates the potential for the developmental supervision model to enhance not only teacher development and students opportunities, but also, to powerfully influence the practice of an experienced supervisor.

A CASE STUDY: PRESCHOOL CLASSROOM WITH A LEEP SUPERVISOR: SUPERVISEE TEAM

A Workplace Childcare Setting

While the public school setting provides an organizational structure with the associated institutional supports inherent in an urban district construct, the developmental supervision model is not dependent upon the external sustenance of a school district. An example of developmental supervision in a workplace-associated daycare center and the supervisor-teacher team of Cindy and Sarah provides evidence for success of the developmental supervision model in a setting separate from a public school district.

The children in this preschool class are all children of graduate students and employees of an urban university. As described by their teacher, Sarah, these students bring a variety of language and culture to the classroom community. The language abilities in this setting range from what Weitzman and Greenberg describe as Stage 3, First Words User to Stage 6, Late Sentence User, (Weitzman & Greenberg, 2202, pp. 41–49). Of interest is that while some of the Stage 3 students are "first word users" in English, they are early or late sentence users in their native languages. The students come from India, China, Japan, Korea, and South America. English speaking students come from a variety of locations from both within and beyond the United States. Often parallel play is engaged in by students who do not readily communicate via a common spoken language. One of the challenges faced by the teachers and supervisor in this setting is providing appropriate supports and models for diversity represented by the student population.

As described by Cindy, the childcare center supervisor, Sarah had a unique career development for a childcare worker. Sarah had been a pre-school teacher at the childcare center for several years and left to pursue her teaching certification and Masters degree in hopes of preparing herself for a public school teaching position. Upon completing her coursework, Sarah "realized that public school was not her calling and returned to the preschool setting." Katz (Caruso and Fawcett, 1999?) defined four stages of preschool teacher development and the training needs for each stage as follows:

Stage 1: *Survival*—Typically lasts through the first year of teaching, when the teacher experiences feelings of self-doubt and insecurity. Teachers need on-site support as well as technical assistance.

Stage 2: *Consolidation*—After making gains during year one, the teacher consolidates those gains and starts to identify tasks and skills to focus on. The supervisor then supports the training relative to these identified areas by providing on-site technical assistance, professional development support from specialists, and collaboration opportunities with consultants and colleagues.

Stage 3: *Renewal*—After teaching for two or three years, some "burnout" can occur and teachers need "renewal" and have a need for joining professional organizations, attending conferences, and having support to enable them to reflect more deeply in analyzing their teaching activities.

Stage 4: *Maturity*—Beyond the fifth year, teachers begin to actively benefit from conference attendance. They enroll in degree programs, attend institutes, assume some leadership roles and contribute to their organizations through writing articles and sharing information. (pp.61–62).

Cindy commented that Sarah's second full year back in preschool, after returning from her Masters program would place her on Stage 2—Consolidation; however, Cindy saw Sarah as exhibiting elements of "renewal." While Sarah was not so much "tired" or "burnt out," Cindy felt Sarah "was feeling as if she had taken a step backwards." Sarah had felt "pressure by friends and family to 'do something' with her degree and certification." Cindy also shared that a colleague who had left to work in a public elementary setting, had recently come back to visit and shared the perceived "plusses" of her new position—the hours, the pay, and the summers off. Sarah was polite, but firm in her conviction that she "now sees early childhood, with enthusiasm, and as a career with a future." Cindy thus sees Sarah appropriately identified as in the "consolidation" stage of development. Cindy stated, "As her supervisor, any article, professional development opportunity, off site visiting that could be offered was offered and will continue to be, not only to support her professional growth, but also to ease and validate her personal dilemma about her decision to return to the early childhood setting." Furthermore, Cindy commented, "As Sarah has moved into her second year, she is significantly more confident in her decision to work with young children, in using the skills learned in her Master's program, and in identifying interesting, appropriate, and stimulating curriculum all around her."

In LEEP, supervisors are presented with a "Framework for Analyzing Classroom Observations." This framework is intended to support supervisors in considering how teachers' practices are complicated by a triad of interacting complexities: the classroom environment, the individual teacher, and the diverse and unique children. The Framework for Analyzing Classroom Observations considers three components:

- *Foundational Knowledge:* The teacher's knowledge of child development and research-based language and literacy instructional practices
- *Beliefs:* A teacher's system of beliefs and values. A teacher's personal beliefs and values can conflict with practices they are responsible for implementing. At times the teacher may not be cognizant of the conflict. At other times an awareness of the conflict may be the source of discord that the teacher is unwilling to or uncomfortable about discussing with a colleague or supervisor. Such discord may then interfere with a teacher's motivation or ability to persevere in attempting to become skilled in those strategies that conflict with the teacher's personal beliefs or values.
- *Complexity of the Innovation:* Some changes in professional practice are considerable and complex in nature. The process is necessarily iterative and teachers can struggle with becoming fluent and feeling competent in engaging in new practice in a variety of ways. Sometimes a teacher may execute new strategies unknowingly superficially, yet judge that she/he has mastered a new practice. Teachers may attempt too much change in too short a time frame and may not be sensitive to the needs of students. In these situations, the eagerness of teachers may result in confusion to students. Ultimately, when students don't respond, the technique or strategy may be misinterpreted as being ineffective.

Cindy employed the Framework when observing Sarah on a number of occasions. In one example, Cindy cited a guided reading lesson of Eric Carle's *Polar Bear, Polar Bear*. Generally, Cindy observed Sarah to be a competent, caring and talented teacher who displayed flexibility in responding to the needs and behaviors of individual children. Despite this, Cindy noted some areas of the lesson that would be appropriate for follow up discussion with Sarah. Specifically, Cindy noted that children were somewhat distracted by the novelty of "animal props" that the teacher was introducing. Cindy observed that only half of the children appeared to "hear" sounds that the teacher had chosen as a focus in this "rhyming" lesson using *Polar Bear, Polar Bear*. Cindy described some children as "squirming in their spots" or appearing "lost." Cindy asserted that the teacher's focus goal of having the children hear the rhyme within the story was not only "unmet," but was also "not relevant" to this first story reading. In light of the framework, Cindy noted that the teacher appeared to be working from her "belief" that students could developmentally "handle" the activity as she had designed it. This was also tied to what she understood in her "fundamental knowledge" about child development. Cindy determined that the teacher had a belief that the particular children in the center are always able to handle novelties (the props) and that this belief was an underlying issue in the lesson execution. Cindy had videotaped the lesson. In the post observation setting, the teacher and Cindy viewed and analyzed the lesson together. Through observation, questioning, reflection, and discussion, Sarah was able to successfully "process the lesson and make decisions for changing the lesson that were more appropriate and more likely to make the lesson more appropriate for the children and for Sarah." She made decisions to introduce the animal sounds first, then the animal props, and finally to integrate these into a story reading. Sarah acknowledged that her typical model for story reading was abandoned in this lesson as she tried to do too much at one time, which contributed to the difficulties with the lesson.

While Cindy felt Sarah had some difficulties in her lesson based upon her beliefs, Sarah believed that she had an understanding of the "complexity of the innovation." In the discussion, Sarah shared that "she had to see the children changing their behavior before she could feel her own change." Cindy interpreted this as evidence validating that Sarah believed her hypothesis was more of an accurate assessment of her personal growth than was her supervisor's hypothesis, which she based on her classroom observation. While Sarah believed she had learned much in her coursework, Cindy still observed many classroom behaviors "that have been consistent since prior to her training . . . For example, relying on preconceived expectations of the students' development . . . Many of her (Sarah's) lessons and presentations are set by this belief."

The video-taping was a powerful conferencing tool. After re-viewing the tape, both Cindy and Sarah were able to come to a closer agreement on how to proceed. They determined that Sarah would review her lesson plan and use it as a model for another videotaped lesson with another book. The videotapes would then be compared and reflected upon.

An important outcome of this experience for Cindy was her reflection upon how much her own beliefs influence her in her role as a supervisor! "The implications of how I view Sarah are based on reviewing years of being a supervisor, years of being part of a support system of fellow supervisors who all view from a similar perspective and a recognition that the old paradigms of supervision may no longer be applicable as we look at the research that supports children's literacy needs and abilities at a pre-school level. As a supervisor, I need to use the Framework for myself, as well as for my staff and to look at the questions about teacher situations, my hypotheses, and most importantly, the verification questions that I ask my staff and myself to support or refute my hypotheses. The other component of this is the need to set a schedule, whether concretely written or just a mental reminder, to revisit the Framework and my hypotheses about this staff, and in this case, Sarah in particular. . . . The Framework forced me to look at Sarah in a more clinical manner than I typically have looked at my staff."

Developmental supervision practices have opened up an entirely new level of planning, reflection and dialogue between a competent supervisor and teacher in this childcare center. After three months time, Cindy reported that Sarah, herself, is in awe of the change in her class. The change in the relationship between the teacher and supervisor has been supportive of the professional growth of both of them and has been the seed for a new perspective and enthusiasm for preschool education. Both Sarah and Cindy share in the excitement of the accomplishments of the students in Sarah's class. As Sarah's supervisor, Cindy faces new challenges that invigorate her own clinical practice, beyond the initial four stages of the cycle of developmental supervision. In the post conference analysis, Cindy must seek new ways to support Sarah's enthusiasm and professional development through courses, workshops and opportunities. Cindy also is determining ways in which Sarah can share what she has learned and experienced by presenting to and sharing with her peers in the center. Cindy commented, "Right now, Sarah and I speak one language and many of her peers speak another." Rolling out the developmental supervision model, coupled with professional development in evidence-based practice is the next step.

A CASE STUDY: PRESCHOOL CLASSROOM WITH A LEEP SUPERVISOR: SUPERVISEE TEAM

Head Start Classroom

Both the public school construct and the workplace childcare facility offer levels of external support and structure that help sustain a program through both material provisions and professional relationships. An example of developmental supervision in a satellite Head Start classroom and the co-teacher team of Carol and Robin exemplify the capacity for success of the developmental supervision model—even in the absence of an on-site supervisor.

Carol and Robin are two Head Start teachers assigned to a satellite classroom in a small community building located in a town approximately 20 miles from the main Head Start site and office. These teachers were committed to participating in the Literacy Environment Enrichment Program and the Developmental Supervision model, despite the fact that they did not have a supervisor who was available to sign up for training as part of a teacher-supervisor team. Fortunately, a Literacy Consultant from the Bureau of Early Childhood of the State Department of Education was interested in professional development in the areas of both the Literacy Environment Enrichment Program and Developmental Supervision and she agreed to serve as a surrogate supervisor for Carol and Robin. After approximately one month of working together, the "supervisor" left the employment of the state department to take an administrative position in a public school system. She intended to maintain her "surrogacy" and team member status with Robin and Carol; however, the responsibilities and demands of her new K-12 supervisory position necessitated her eventual resignation from her work with the team. Determined to succeed, Robin and Carol persevered alone and eventually were able to connect with a supervisor from a neighboring school system who committed to supporting them and serving as their distant surrogate supervisor for the model.

During the interlude in which Carol and Robin were without direct supervisory support, they had each other to serve as peers. Caruso and Fawcett (1999, p.155) suggest that colleagues can actively support each other by participating in a peer-supervision relationship. In this model, teachers observe the teaching of their peers and engage in reflection and mutual feedback, while building colleagueship. Peer-supervision, in design, is intended to allow a supervisor or director to engage in a variety of other significant tasks; however, in this situation, Robin and Carol willingly and independently assumed this option rather than face losing the opportunity to participate in training and professional development opportunities. Their original surrogate supervisor helped Carol and Robin identify areas in their practice that were in need of improvement. She was concerned, at first, that the teachers seemed primarily interested in learning new activities to take and put into practice in their classroom, as is sometimes the case for teachers attending in-service trainings. Her expressed hope was that Robin ad Carol's conference time with her would transform their attitudes about their own learning and that through reflecting on their practice they would develop a sense of life-long learning. She felt this in turn might be useful to them in the future as they reflect on their practice collaboratively as teachers. As long time Head Start teachers, she felt they had tremendous classroom experience; however, she perceived they may not have had much experience with someone critiquing their work.

She deemed it to be extremely important to be able to convey to each of them that she had respect for their role as teachers and that she wanted to create an atmosphere that would lead them to realize that they can take ownership for much of the observation process. She felt it was important to be extremely clear and well-prepared in understanding the developmental supervision process so that she could support them. Her hope was that the teachers would be able to transfer this process to their own decision making as they teach, observe and assess, and plan lessons with their students.

Another important outcome that the surrogate supervisor targeted was the creation of a climate that would encourage the teachers to maintain a level of professional dialogue that would continue to support their growth together. She believed that this would provide the children in their classes with rich learning opportunities. These initial thoughts and actions taken by the surrogate supervisor were likely instrumental in preparing Carol and Robin to carry-on after her unexpected departure.

The surrogate shared her perspective on the development of a supervisor in the developmental supervision model. She stated, "I like to think about this type of growth as a professional as an analogy for learning to ride a bike. Initially as the 'novice' we are hesitant and unsure of our selves and reach out for support that might keep us balanced. We hesitate to ride down hills and we watch others around us very carefully before moving out ahead on the new road."

Furthermore, she stated, "As supervisors gain more experience, the second phase of development, the 'transition' phase, the supervisor is more apt to be a little more assured and is willing to take new risks. The supervisor will still need to keep her eye on the road and may continue to rely on some of those supports needed earlier to maintain balance. But the supervisor at this stage is more willing to extend responsibilities and use the knowledge of previous experiences and feels more comfortable and will begin to enjoy the ride." She stated that she appreciated that supervisors at this stage "are more apt to recognize the individual abilities of staff because they are not as focused on their own development and can now look to other's development. They are the more secure 'bike rider' and now are more willing to 'ride ahead' and 'ride along side of' in a leadership role that both guides and nudges."

In the next stage or third stage, she continued, "The 'mature' supervisor becomes the experienced leader ready to set out on a 'bike trek'. The supervisor will be able to lead the way by modeling the necessary skills and behaviors for a successful 'ride' and will confidently direct others to the path that needs to be followed. They may even have several ideas, resources and supports in their 'backpack of experience' that they now acquired in their own journey and development as a leader. This person is a more confident supervisor and is willing to offer support and guidance to others but will also recognize the benefit of learning and gaining feedback from those for whom they work (parents) and who work for them (staff)."

Thus, when the surrogate left, Carol and Robin had a foundation upon which to build and support each other until they could engage with another supervisor model. Initially these teachers had been unsure and a bit uncomfortable about their potential for success in tackling the task of learning new literacy strategies and engaging in developmental supervision. These teachers were treated with respect and as professionals by their surrogate supervisor and gained knowledge, confidence and an increased level of self esteem. Not only were they highly successful in learning and implementing high quality early literacy strategies in their classrooms, but they were equally victorious in accomplishing the goals of developmental supervision in their peer-supervision model. When they met with their subsequent surrogate supervisor, she was amazed at the quality of the work Robin and Carol had produced—in their classroom practice, in their knowledge base, and as evidenced in their videotapes and portfolios. The students in Carol and Robin's classes showed high levels of engagement in a variety of literacy activities. Carol and Robin found their planning for and reflecting upon lessons became highly dependent upon assessing work generated by the students and observations and documentation of student work. They both expressed that planning and teaching was easier and made more sense since they learned more about documentation and reflection. Working so closely as "peer-supervisors" was instrumental in changing the content and quality of the discussions they had about their students and their classroom space.

Carol and Robin's experience was so highly positive and confidence fostering that they had a desire to enroll in additional advanced training and educational programs. The developmental supervision process was indeed a powerful model for these two early childhood teachers. After decades of teaching, they were newly enthusiastic and eager to continue their personal learning journey.

As seen by these three very different teams of teachers and teacher-supervisors, developmental supervision is a powerful model for supporting teachers in their professional growth journey. Clearly, success is not limited to novice teachers, and new supervisors, nor is it limited to "conventional" teams. Not only did the teachers entrenched in the developmental supervision model grow, but the supervisors did as well. In each case, teachers were more observant of and reflective about their students. The documentation the teachers kept on the week to week student activities and progress demonstrated that the students greatly benefited from the support and professional growth their teachers experienced by being involved in the process of developmental supervision.

REFERENCES

Caruso, J. & Fawcett (1999). *Supervision in early childhood education.* New York: Teachers College Press.

Kame'enui, E. J., Simmons, D. C., Baker, S., Chard, D. J., Dickson, S. V., Gunn, B., Smith, S. B., Sprick, M., & Lin, S. J. (1997). Effective strategies for teaching beginning reading. In E. J. Kame'enui, & D. W. Carnine (Eds.), *Effective Teaching Strategies That Accommodate Diverse Learners.* Columbus, OH: Merrill.

National Research Council (1998). *Preventing reading difficulties in young children.* Washington, DC: National Academy Press.

Noddings, N. (1999). Caring and competence. In G. Griffen (Ed.), *The education of teachers* (pp. 205–220). Chicago: National Society of Education.

Schickendanz, J. (1999). *Much more than the ABCs.* Washington, D.C.: NAEYC.

Torgesen, J. K., & Bryant, B. T. (1994). *Phonological awareness training for reading.* Austin, TX: Pro-ed.

Weitzman, E. & Greenberg, J. (2002). *Learning language and loving it.* Toronto, Ontario, Canada: The Hanen Centre.

Yopp, H. K. (1992). Developing phonemic awareness in young children. *Reading Teacher, 45*(9), 696–703.

Chapter Four

Scaffolding Early Literacy Development

Janet Price and Norris M. Haynes

INTRODUCTION

Building and nurturing relationships in the preschool setting is essential to scaffolding all learning, and in this case, language and literacy learning. With the recent new understandings of early brain development we are now more aware than ever of the need for learning to take place in the larger context of developing strong, healthy self-esteem. "Each achievement—language and learning, social development, the emergence of self-regulation—occurs in the context of close relationships with others." (Shonkoff & Phillips, 2000, p. 225). This means that attention must be focused in the classroom on supporting positive social-emotional development through building strong relationships. To present topical information, such as literacy, in a vacuum can sometimes result in an inability to make meaning of the information presented. This is because learning, especially at the preschool age level, must connect with one's experience and understanding of reality. Through an ever-growing array of life experiences, both at school and at home, new knowledge has an opportunity to build on current understandings. Only when new information has meaning in young children's lives can they truly benefit and become engaged in the learning process.

   In this chapter the authors look at strategies to support the scaffolding of early literacy development through building and strengthening relationships. It is essential to keep in focus where literacy development fits into the broader picture of building competence. "When children are feeling competent—when their minds, bodies and emotions are in the proper gear and they are functioning well—they are ready to learn." (Kaiser and Rasminsky, 1999). It is helpful to look at strategies to encourage positive relationships in various formats that occur in the classroom. Through building a positive relationship between teacher and child, children have a safe environment where they can try new things, building on current knowledge and abilities to support them in taking the next step in understanding. One needs to look at supporting positive relationships with peers—interactions where new learning can occur, can be integrated into current understandings, and can build towards next steps in understanding. Finally, one must look at strategies to encourage positive relationships between families and professionals, a partnership that can increase the potential for scaffolding to occur in early literacy development.

BUILDING POSITIVE TEACHER-CHILD RELATIONSHIPS

Relationship-building between teacher and child is key to supporting children's opportunities for engagement in learning that are made available in the classroom. Getting to know each child as a unique person and finding the positive characteristics and traits that each child brings to the group is essential. "Teacher-child relationships play a significant role in influencing young children's social and emotional development" (Ostrosky, & Jung, 2004). One positive outcome of getting to know a child is that the teacher learns about what interests the child. This means that the teacher can create a common language by encouraging the child to talk about what interests him/her. Then the teacher can utilize that common language to engage in more complex conversations and verbal exchanges. The teacher may offer books on the topic of interest, which is a more meaningful way to draw the child to engage in literacy experiences; as compared to offering random books that a child might not have a base of reference for in terms of engaging with the book content. By getting to know a child the teacher discovers how that child learns. That knowledge can then inform the teacher about the best way of introducing new learning in formats that will best engage the child. Does this child learn best when he/she has the opportunity to sit back and watch what is happening around him/her before being expected to join in? Does another child learn best when he/she can jump in and become involved with the material immediately? Does one child like to explore the written word alone in a quiet space, while another is more likely to engage when the book is read aloud in a group? Discovering each child's most responsive mode of learning is critical in encouraging success in literacy development. Developing a relationship with a child offers the teacher the opportunity to observe that child's learning style and needs. Included in the process of building strong teacher-child relationships is taking children's emotions seriously. (Plattner, 2003).

A key element to building positive relationships with children is when the teacher is able to communicate a respect for that child's family and culture, both the culture from which the child and family originate and the culture in which she is being raised. Finding ways to celebrate these aspects of a child's identity is an important aspect of getting to know each child and making the classroom a safe and familiar environment. When a child feels safe, and is seen and understood by his/her teacher and in the classroom, her self-esteem and self-confidence grow. The child then has a strong foundation for taking the important steps of exploring new learning.

An important strategy for teachers to build positive relationships with children is to have positive assumptions about each and every child with whom the teacher works (Education Development Center, 1999). If it is assumed that a child cannot do something then it would be difficult for a teacher to encourage success, or to help a child believe that he/she can. Some children have more confidence and are more self-assured. Other children are less confident and more diffident. These are the children who need greater support and encouragement to engage meaningfully and productively in the learning process. It is essential to put specific learning into the broader context of growth and development. As recent brain development research has shown, social-emotional development provides the foundation for growth in specific learning areas, such as language and literacy development. Social-emotional development includes attitudes toward learning and actual learning directed behaviors. Children cannot learn and teachers cannot teach when challenging behaviors are taking center stage. It helps, therefore, to consider some additional strategies for supporting social-emotional development and encouraging positive behaviors.

Teachers have the opportunity to encourage appropriate student behavior through their own body language, and by listening attentively and asking questions. Teachers should pay attention to what they communicate through their body language when interacting with children for whom they have positive feelings. Then, they should notice how their body language changes when they interact with children for whom they do not have such positive feelings. How close to the child do you stand? Do you get at eye-level? Notice how stiff or relaxed the body becomes. Notice the movement and positioning of the hands, clenched, open, reaching out to assist or on the hip. As teachers start to become more conscious of what their body language communicates, they can control the messages they send to children. Listening attentively and asking open-ended questions can support a child's sense of competence, which will ultimately scaffold specific learning, including language and literacy. When "children's minds, bodies, and emotions are in the proper gear and they are functioning well, they are ready to learn." (Kaiser and Rasminsky, 1999). It is important for teachers to pay attention to the questions they ask. Are they questions that request a yes or no answer? Or do the questions encourage conversations that require thinking, wondering and discussing?

There is an underlying message to these strategies, which is the realization that the teachers have the power to change children's behavior by changing their own, whether it is their assumptions, the way they communicate through body language, or how well they listen and learn to appreciate the unique strengths of each child. Literacy development needs to occur in the context of meaningful relationships. Strengthening attachment is essential for children to make broader meaning of what they learn. Children's emotional attachments to the teacher, learning situation and material taught can motivate them to master the use of language

ENCOURAGING POSITIVE RELATIONSHIPS WITH PEERS

Children share ideas, ask questions, and solve problems through play. In that context the written word becomes relevant. Play that encourages language and literacy development is optimal when it occurs through peer relationships and interactions. Besides creating opportunities for language development play also builds a child's social-emotional competence. So, it is a critical feature of the preschool classroom to provide these opportunities. Teachers are able to support peer connections through how they structure play opportunities in the classroom. In planning for this the teacher brings what she knows about each child's present level of cognitive and social development, how each child approaches learning, and how to structure the classroom environment to best encourage cooperative play interactions. It might come as a surprise to be talking about play in the midst of our larger focus on literacy development. Play takes center stage at this point. "Play has been found to contribute to several areas of development, including social, emotional, and cognitive development, including literacy." (Zigler, 2004). For young children, learning develops in the context of play. Gaining new skills and understanding is most useful when that learning has meaning to the child. Through play children will exhibit their current understanding and will demonstrate what context is meaningful to them. For many children play skills come naturally. For others they need support to gain those interactive skills. Co-playing (Scarlet, 2004) is one strategy for supporting that learning with children. In this scenario, teachers "co-play" with the child. By entering into the play with the child, the teacher has opportunities to model play skills, to help children connect with each other and with the activity, and to build skills for learning how to initiate play. The teacher or other adults in the classroom can encourage collaboration among the children, including children in play at whatever level of participation they are able to access. Plus, teachers can extend play and enhance language opportunities and literacy activities resulting from this level of play (Stacey, 2000). Teachers can model extended conversations, keeping dialog alive for a number of interchanges back and forth through a focus on the play.

FORGING SUCCESSFUL PARTNERSHIPS WITH PARENTS AND TEACHERS

Educators have been aware for many years that the best way to support children's learning is through family involvement in children's education. Head Start is a fine example of a national early childhood education system with a long-standing commitment to family-school partnerships. The inclusion of family reaches to every aspect of the school's functioning and supporting children's school success. In recent years this goal for early childhood programs nation-wide has been put to the test as more families have less time and energy to bring to in-class involvement. Rather than give in to discouragement about the fading of traditional family involvement, it is now necessary for educators to change their paradigm regarding what parent/teacher partnerships could look like, while never losing sight of the goal of encouraging such a partnership.

It is interesting and possibly surprising to realize that teachers and parents have the same goals for their children's education: ensuring that each child is a contributing member of the class and grows in all areas of development. Starting with that understanding can help to build this partnership, as teachers and parents work together to discover what kind of classroom participation and connection is possible for a particular family. Parents deserve teachers' respect for doing the best that they can. As with the children in the classroom, each family and each member within that particular family is an individual with unique abilities and challenges that are brought to the parenting relationship. Just as the teacher individualizes for each child in the classroom, strategies for family involvement need to also be individualized, with a "tool kit" of possible engagement at the teacher's disposal. This toolkit can include some of the following strategies: (1) make a commitment at the beginning of the year to set up a format for ongoing communication that feels workable for each family, and (2) decide in the fall, or when that child first joins the classroom, what works best for that family regarding sharing home/school information and updates. By creating a communication system at the very beginning of the year, the teacher has the opportunity to build a positive relationship with the family. That means finding positive observations and comments to share, an essential aspect of connecting with a family. When a positive parent-school relationship is created it is much easier to discuss concerns if they should arise, from either the family or school. Again, relationships are key to supporting a child's learning. A line of communication between home and school that is more regular (daily, weekly, bi-weekly) and less formal than quarterly parent-teacher conferences, provides opportunities for the school to match suggested literacy activities to what is possible and available in the home. Such communication supports the ability to carry over the learning at school into the home. Extended learning opportunities are a powerful tool for building competence. Teachers should share with the family various options for ongoing communication, including a journal sent back and forth from school and home with entries made by the teachers and parents, weekly phone calls, updates at drop off or pick up. It helps for teachers to be creative and to welcome input from parents about what form and timing of information sharing works best for them.

Opportunities for parent involvement can range from volunteering in the class on a regular basis; one-time visits into the classroom to share customs from the family's culture, or family rituals or careers; participating on school committees, or other participating in other decision-making opportunities; or helping out from home by gathering materials needed for projects. Communication between teachers and parents is what enhances positive experiences for the child and ultimately scaffolds learning. In approaching parents teachers can utilize similar strategies used for interacting positively with the children in the class. This is because respectful communication strategies are universal for all human interactions. These include:

- Prepare for meetings with family members. Think about what you are going to say so your comments are specific, respectful and positive;
- Listen attentively, rather than using that time to formulate you next "gems of wisdom";
- Respond to the need within the parent's message;
- State the positive first;
- Deliver your thoughts in a way that is calm and non-threatening;
- Use language that is empowering for the family;
- Share information about the child in a positive light. That means share the successes first, then any challenges. Challenges shared need to be followed with ideas for addressing these challenges. Include the parents in this dialogue, as they often have essential information to provide that can shed

light on the source of the challenge and possible solutions, or next steps. This is an opportunity to create a true sense of partnership as you look together at possible solutions;
- Model the kinds of interactions that you hope to have together—respectful, collaborative, recognizing any feelings that are shared without judgment. (Stacey, 2000, p. 15).

Forging a partnership takes time. Building that relationship means being patient and consistent in the approach so that trust can grow between the two members of this partnership (parents and teachers) by following the strategies listed above. By building positive relationships with parents starting at the beginning of the year there is much more opportunity for teachers and parents to learn valuable information that can ultimately have a positive outcome for children's learning. Children understand that home and school both care about their learning. Scaffolding learning can occur both at school and at home, through effective communication between home and school.

BRINGING IT ALL TOGETHER THROUGH STORYTELLING AND STORY ACTING

Finally, it helps to look at a unique approach to a well-known and loved activity that is often included in the classroom curriculum to encourage language and literacy development—storytelling and story acting. This activity is able to pull together all that has been discussed in this chapter, as the process of storytelling and story acting offer opportunities to build positive relationships—between child and teacher, among peers, and between school and home. This then strongly supports the scaffolding of literacy learning. In the most common format children are encouraged to re-tell stories that have been told or read to them. They might have the opportunity to act them out. Through this wonderful use of storytelling multiple aspects of literacy are presented and encouraged.

In the context of scaffolding literacy development through building relationships we are going to consider another approach to storytelling. Vivian Paley's work in this arena for example, *Wally's Stories,* has brought this approach to storytelling to the forefront of strategies for strengthening relationships and scaffolding learning (Paley, 1981). With this approach the story comes from within the child. Whatever the child dictates becomes the story. It can be as simple as this three-year-old's story: "There was a little bear that he standed on his head." (Paley, 1999).Those words are written down. They become the story, and that story, word for word, is read aloud while acted out by peers in the class. It is a process that appears to be quite simple, both to set up and to carry out. Yet the possibility for important connections and understandings to occur is profound When a child shares what is on his/her mind, in whatever language format that he/she is able to, and those words and thoughts are accepted exactly as they are, this can be an important moment of self-esteem building. The teacher takes those words and commits them to paper, which further demonstrates the power of one's words. Finally when those words are acted out by one's peers, then that child is seen and celebrated by both his/her teacher and classmates. Relationships are strengthened and literacy development is encouraged.

Let's describe this storytelling process in more detail using *The Boy Who Would Be a Helicopter* (Paley, 1999) as an example. First, the teacher chooses an area of the classroom for the stage. He/she can mark that territory in some manner, such as with masking tape. Next he/she introduces this activity by gathering the class to sit around the border of the stage. He/she explains that they are each going to have the opportunity to tell a story and act it out. He/she asks for a volunteer. As the volunteer tells his/her story the teacher writes it down on paper in front of the group. When the child is done he/she reads the story back to the child. The story has been recorded word for word, even if it is not in complete sentences, or doesn't have the traditional parts of a story—beginning, middle, and ending. This in fact is often the case with young (chronologically or developmentally) preschool children. The teacher asks the child if he/she would like to have his/her story acted out. If he/she agrees the teacher picks children to play the various parts, letting the author choose which part he/she would like to be, if any. The story acting occurs.

Now that the class has seen how this process works, the teacher announces that there will be a center during Free Choice time where individuals can come over and tell the teacher their story. The teacher asks to see who would like to do so and writes down their names. It is important that whatever stories are told on a specific day are acted out the same day. What is important for a child to share at one moment might have lost its meaning by tomorrow. This timing captures the emotion and intent of telling that story at that moment. It is also fine for a child to not choose to tell a story. One of the ways that this process embraces each child wherever they are in their development (including social-emotional, language, and literacy) is that there are multiple ways to be involved, and each is a crucial aspect of the storytelling process. For every story told three forms of participation are needed: the storyteller, the actors, and the audience! So every child will immediately belong and feel needed to make this work. Then, as the year progresses, and the class becomes more familiar with this storytelling and acting process, children who were quiet and chose every time to be in the audience will start to help with acting out a classmate's story, and eventually realize that it is also safe to tell their story, whatever the format—whether just a few words or a detailed story!

This process provides unique opportunities for supporting social-emotional development. Children are encouraged to tell a story about whatever is on their minds. Their story is respected and honored by writing it down. It is further honored by having classmates act it out and other peers be the audience and witness their story. This process provides rich opportunities for the teacher to get to know the children in ways that are real and often intimate. Many of the story themes are carried over into play time. This encourages positive peer interactions because the children know more about each other and have already collaborated on acting out each other's stories on the stage. Children with limited language can still participate. Single word sentences can be written down and acted out. Children with little or no language can still be part of other children's stories as they are acted out.

Other exciting outcomes of this approach to storytelling and story acting are the conversations and sharing that are possible at parent-teacher conferences. When teachers share with parents the stories that their children have created, parents are usually proud and often touched to hear what their children are thinking. It provides openings for rich and open dialogue between them about children's development in many areas. Parents feel that their children's teachers are getting to know their children in real and meaningful ways, thus building trust between parents and teachers. This whole process provides a supportive and stimulating context that encourages language and literacy development among children.

CONCLUSION

Building positive relationships is essential to scaffolding early literacy development. Children's learning happens in the larger context of life experiences. Life explorations occur in the context of relationships. Building relationships strengthens children's social-emotional competence, a precursor to academic learning. As documented in this chapter, relationships between teacher and child, among children, and between a child's family and the child's teacher, all deserve conscious, focused attention and nurturing. The strategies for building these relationships are often similar in approach no matter which relationship is the focus. Strengthening relationships helps to nurture strong, healthy and positive learning environments and to produce positive learning outcomes.

STRATEGIES FOR SCAFFOLDING EARLY LITERACY DEVELOPMENT DESCRIBED IN THIS CHAPTER

1. *Strategies for Building Relationships with Children*:
   - Pay attention to each individual child
   - Give children one-on-one positive attention
   - Know what interests each child and talk to the child about that interest
   - Respect each child's approach to situations and people
   - Show respect for children's culture, linguistics, and religious beliefs
   - Empowering assumptions
   - Storytelling and story-acting
2. *Strategies for Encouraging Positive Peer Interactions*
   - Use your body language to send positive messages
   - Listen attentively
   - Respond to the need within the child's message
   - The essential role of play and co-playing in the classroom
   - Storytelling and story-acting
3. *Strategies for Forging Successful Family/Teacher Partnerships*
   - Create formats for ongoing communication between school and home
   - Provide opportunities for school involvement that meet the needs of the family
   - Storytelling and story-acting

REFERENCES

Education Development Center, Newton, M.A. (1999).*Supporting children with challenging behaviors: Relationships are key Washington DC:* US Department of Health and Human Services.

Kaiser, B. & Rasminsky, J. S. (1999*). Meeting the challenge: Effective strategies for challenging behaviors in early childhood environments,* Ottawa: Canadian Child Care Federation.

Ostrosky, M. M. & Jung, E. Y.(2004). *Building positive teacher-child relationships.* Nashville: The Center on the Social and Emotional Foundations for Early Learning, January, 2004.

Paley, V. G., (1999). *The boy who would be a helicopter: The uses of storytelling in the classroom,* Cambridge: Harvard University Press.

Paley, V. G. (1981). *Wally's stories: Conversations in the kindergarten.* Cambridge: Harvard University Press.

Plattner, L. (2003).*Granting children their emotions.* ExchangeEveryDay. http://www.childcareexchange.com

Scarlett, W. G. (2004). *Connecting: Friendship in the lives of young children and their teachers.*ExchangeEveryDay. http://www.childcareexchange.com

Shonkoff, J. P. & Phillips, D. A. (2000). *From neurons to neighborhoods*, (pp. 225–266). Washington DC:National Academy Press.

Stacey, S. (March 2000). *Facilitating collaborations among children.* Exchange EveryDay. http://www.childcareexchange.com

Zigler, E. (2004).*Play under siege.* New Haven: 21 Community News, Winter 2004.

Chapter Five

Professional Development

Nancy Marano

Prompted by various reform movements, government mandates (No Child Left Behind, 2001) and professional organization position statements (NAEYC, 1999) targeting teachers as central to student achievement as well as school improvement, over the last two decades, researchers have focused on many of the complex aspects of professional development or more specifically on teacher learning (Chard, 2004; Fullan, 1991; Hawley & Valli, 1999; Richardson, 1990; Little, 1999; Showers, 1990). For example, Fullan (1991) in his comprehensive study of educational change argued that the role of the teacher should be considered the focal point for any kind of school change or instructional intervention. Teachers, Fullan reminds us, must be in the forefront of the reform. Indeed, they must believe that changing their teaching will serve pragmatic purposes as well as be worthwhile for their students. Teachers necessarily must not only buy into, they must take the lead on, the changes to be made (Cochran-Smith & Lytle, 1992).

In order for teachers to become committed to reform, they should be certain that the instructional changes will be good for their students, easily implemented, and have clearly successful outcomes (Fullan, 1991; Guskey, 1986). The lack of success of many reform movements in the past, particularly ones aiming for the development of child-centered forms of education, may be linked to a failure to focus on teacher knowledge (Darling-Hammond, 1990). Essential to school or instructional change is the provision for appropriate and productive opportunities of teacher learning where teachers believe they will receive ongoing support from colleagues, administrators, and the institution (Hawley & Valli, 1999; Little, 1999). Thus, teachers are powerful agents influencing the success or failure of professional development activities and in turn student success. However, the literature on teacher learning and instructional change from the last two decades has indicated that the relationship between quality teaching and successful outcomes is complex.

In this chapter our aim is to examine the best practices and contexts for fostering teacher learning through professional development in early literacy learning. We begin by presenting the features of professional development contexts and activities that have, according to the literature, emerged as those offering the richest opportunities for teacher learning and change. The reader will note that these features are consistent with sociocultural theory, including the constructs of the social construction of knowledge mediated by cultural tools (Vygotsky, 1987; Wertsch, 1998) and the theories of activity (Leont'ev, 1979) and participation (Rogoff, 1990).

WORTHWHILE FEATURES OF PRODUCTIVE PROFESSIONAL DEVELOPMENT CONTEXTS

Professional Development Contexts Are Collaborative

The teacher learning literature, both empirical and theoretical, reflects an important tension within the culture of teaching: the individual vs. the community, that is, the private vs. the public in teaching. This tension is born from what seems to be teachers' natural desire for an independent and autonomous privacy in their classrooms while simultaneously wishing for collaboration and collegiality (Hargreaves, 1994; Little, 1990; 1992; Little & McLaughlin, 1993: Lortie, 1977). Virginia Richardson (2001) has more recently argued that this conflict is uniquely American and common to tensions in our democratic society between the public and the private. Much of the extant literature on effective teacher learning examines this tension and provides arguments in favor of the importance of promoting collaboration, collegiality and a sense of professional community for teachers as learners because, in spite of this independent and autonomous streak, teachers themselves report that collegial contexts and relationships are most productive for their learning (Cochran-Smith & Lytle, 1992; 1999; Foorman & Moats, 2004; Lefevre & Richardson, 2002; Little, 1990; Palincsar, et al, 1998; Richardson, 1994). While acknowledging some of the difficulties and tensions in collaboration, much of the literature supports the notion that collaborative contexts where teachers come together to discuss and inquire into new knowledge as they connect it to their experience and expertise provide the most fruitful opportunities for learning. Judith Warren Little's work (1990; 1999) comes to mind in particular because she examined the interplay between collaboration and individual autonomy. Little (1990) urged a focus on collaboration and interdependence through "joint work" (p. 519) and argued that if the content of the collaborative work is substantive and engaging and shared understanding and goals of inquiry into children's learning are promoted, that interdependence would indeed be supported (Little, 1999). Furthermore, the work of Palincsar and her associates (1998) illuminates in a practical sense how collegiality and the "diverse expertise" (p. 8) contributed by all the members of "teacher community of practice" were both essential to the ongoing work of the community (see Palincsar, Magnusson, Marano, Ford, & Brown, 1998). Similarly, a few years earlier, working from the understanding that a sense of community was essential to teacher learning, Grossman (1992) considered learning within the contexts of Professional Development Schools. In these schools, all participants, experienced teachers, novice teachers, preservice teachers, and students are viewed as learners. University faculty, school faculty and administration, interns and student teachers came together in this program to foster various aspects of teacher, as well as, student learning. For example, cooperating teachers who worked with student teachers reported that having the student in their classroom positioned them to reflect on their own teaching. Grossman reported, "Teachers may rethink their actions subsequent to a discussion with a novice teacher or may come to understand more clearly the connections, or lack of connections, between their goals and their action" (p. 185). At the heart of these interactions is a sense of collegiality.

More recently, the National Research Council's Committee on the Prevention of reading Difficulties in Young Children (Snow, Griffin, & Burns, 1998) proposed several recommendations toward building collegiality among educators with common interests and varying degrees of expertise. From their reviews of early literacy research, the panel members suggested criteria for professional development contexts that would be most effective and supportive of early childhood teachers as they developed understandings about early literacy contexts and strategies.

We consider the possibilities of supporting and encouraging teacher research discussion groups as well as fostering school-university relationships with the goal of creating joint study groups. With these kinds of long term participant structures, the panel suggests that the teacher learning outcomes will result in "more long-lasting changes than do common one-shot workshops." (p. 292)

In their paper outlining the importance of research based practices in early reading instruction, specifically in the Texas Reading Initiative and the authors' research projects in Houston and Washington, D.C., Foorman and Moats (2004) signal the important role of collaboration for teachers in the professional development programs associated with these reading intervention projects. The participating teachers From the Washington, D.C. program reported that in addition to their own knowledge growth in early literacy learning, they believed that their successful learning was a result of "the availability of material support, and enjoyment of a supportive, collaborative professional context in which learning was rewarding, reciprocal, useful, and exciting." (p. 55)

It was the facilitators of a professional development program who were of interest to LeFevre and Richardson (2002) in their project investigating the perceived role of facilitators in successful professional development programs. This investigation was part of the inquiry into professional development and policy, Inquiry 3 of the Center for Improvement of Early Reading Achievement (CIERA). LeFevre and Richardson analyzed collaboration as represented in the relationships between the professional development program facilitators and the participating teachers. The researchers studied the roles of the facilitators and teachers across five programs working toward reform in literacy instruction: Success for All, Literacy Program, Eclectic School Program, State Standards Project. The facilitators of these programs were asked to describe the characteristics of a successful professional development program. They were also asked about dilemmas they faced. The researchers found that there were common beliefs about the characteristics of successful staff development across the programs. The facilitators agreed that the use of time was critical, that building of community among the teachers including a sense of trust and ability to share was essential. Dilemmas were also noted, and interestingly, the common dilemmas reported by the facilitators had to do with the conflict between establishing trust while pushing teachers to take risks and critique each other. Another dilemma was in striving to balance each teacher's autonomy with externally driven directives of the programs as well as interesting tensions connected with who would be "setting the agenda," the teachers or the facilitators.

Suggesting that shared understanding can emerge from collaboration, Strickland and Barnett (2003) in their review of the literature of professional development programs focused particularly on literacy interventions for young children. The authors found that in addition to successful programs resulting from the "existence of clearly defined parameters of performance for staff" (p. 113), they also learned that "common beliefs and understandings about early childhood learning and teaching" (p. 114) shared by the teachers are essential to success and maintenance of best practices.

Taylor and Pearson (2004) in a three year study also supported by CIERA School Change Project, reviewed professional development programs supporting literacy intervention strategies for teachers. One of the goals of the CIERA School Change project was to introduce reading reform in a variety of schools across the United States. The professional development for teachers in these schools was structured around the following principles: 1) The literacy interventions were focused solely on the needs of the students in the school; 2) The teachers collaborated on ways to bring instruction to the students as well as what their own learning experiences would be; and 3) The content of the knowledge presented to the teachers would be based on research in "reading instruction, school reform, effective teachers, and parent partnerships" (p. 174). From this study, the authors concluded that while the presentation and implementation of research based practice is important,

> [We] have learned that we must pay as much attention to the learning environments of teachers as we do to the learning environments of students. Teachers in the School Change Project were successful when collectively they took advantage of the opportunity to learn or refine and reflect on research-based instructional techniques through a collaborative study group model . . . Study groups and the sharing of study group success helped teachers develop better communication and a common instructional language across grades. (p. 179)

Finally, Chard (2004) took a methodological perspective in an investigation of professional development in reading instruction intervention for struggling readers. Applying Gilbert's Conceptual Framework of Systemic and Personal Variables related to Professional Development, Chard examined the ways in which the personal variables intersect with teacher learning in reading instruction. Using the conceptual framework, Chard was able to foreground the complexities of professional development contexts. Gilbert's frame views system and person variables across three variable types: Information, Instrumentation, and Motivation. Chard matches system and person variables to each type explicating exactly what the components are that, for example, are critical to teachers' self report of their learning and experiences in the professional development activity. Citing motivation as critical to teachers' success in a professional development program, Chard explained that teachers who have sustained and continued to implement newly learned instructional practices report that among other factors that contributed to this sustainability, that "Development of a support network that included other teachers using the instructional practice" (p. 181) was important. In addition, "Teachers particularly valued having other teachers to share ideas and resolve problems." (p. 181)

To return to the tension between individual and community, researchers who have studied collaboration and teacher collegiality (Little, 1990; 1992; Grimmet & Crehan, 1992) as a process for teacher learning and growth have raised questions about the possibility of diluting or dissolving teachers' voices when they are mixed together in an effort to come to shared understanding while collaborating. They have especially raised questions about whether there can be room for creativity and innovation when the voices of a community speak as one. They have suggested that there may be occasions when collegiality actually stifles new ideas and may perpetuate the status quo. In response, Little (1990) urged that we encourage teachers to focus on the content of the collaboration and the creation of interdependence while maintaining an awareness of the culture of privacy and individualism that may be embedded in teachers' professional lives. Thus, if the content of teachers' joint work is substantive, engaging, and grounded in inquiry into student learning as a shared goal, interdependence can flourish. (Little, 1999).

The construct of collaboration in professional development, while essential as a feature of the learning context, may be a double-edged sword. The members of a professional community often seek a sense of collegiality/collaboration; however, collegiality among members may not naturally support striving toward growth and innovation. While these collegial relationships appear to be important to the process of teacher learning, they also require careful attention and continual refinement.

EFFECTIVE PROFESSIONAL DEVELOPMENT PROGRAMS TAKE PLACE OVER TIME WITH ONGOING SUPPORT CONTRIBUTING TO SUSTAINABILITY

A second feature essential to fostering teacher learning in a professional development setting is ongoing support. Ongoing support is characterized by long term, collaborative relationships with professional development facilitators who work with teachers and continue to provide time, materials, and intellectual motivation that contribute to teacher renewal and sustainability of the instructional interventions. Teachers often express the importance of professional development activities that are experienced over time and are built on relationships with the facilitators, and that short, one-day workshops on discrete topics are simply not meaningful to them or to their practice (Richardson, 1990; Palincsar, et al, 1998; Grossman, 1992). Questions of maintenance or sustainability arise whenever professional development programs are analyzed or reflected upon. Indeed, along with examining the effects on student learning, professional development programs are often evaluated by whether the newly implemented learning strategies are maintained and sustained over time, and it appears that ongoing support is an integral factor to maintenance.

The Committee on Preventing Reading Difficulties (Snow, Griffin, & Burns, 1998) clearly argue that teacher learning for teachers of young children should not end at graduation nor should it be centered only on university courses. The authors explain that learning for teachers who are novice or seasoned is best thought of as "ongoing support from colleagues and specialists, as well as regular opportunities for self-examination and reflection" (p. 10). They suggest that there can be productive intellectual work that emerges for all parties who are part of a relationship that includes university faculty, school faculty and staff. These kinds of experiences can have a strong influence on the development of exemplary teachers.

Also, Strickland and Barnett's (2003) review suggests that effective professional development affords rich experiences when it is provided over time, is a well defined model that evolves, and is refined over time as participants reflect on their changing practice while the "fidelity to existing practice may be maintained" (p. 114). Stahl and Yaden (2004) in their review of CIERA studies focusing on early literacy interventions also argue for time in the structure of professional development experiences proposing simply that "short term teacher training interventions or a new curriculum will not yield long term results without a sustained, systematic program of staff development that teachers feel that they own." (p. 152). This sense of ownership calls to mind Fullan's (1991) argument that any kind of intervention or change requires teacher commitment and investment in the program before it can go forward. Because early literacy and language development in young children is complex and the introduction of new techniques and teaching strategies requires acceptance, agreement, and common understanding for all concerned, providing time is essential (Stahl & Yaden, 2004). Foorman and Moats (2004) agree with the need for professional development programs to be structured with plenty of time provided and a "continuous presence" (p. 55) supporting the learning and implementation of research-based instructional strategies and enhancing the potential for sustainability.

Dickinson and McCabe (2001) presented a comprehensive explanation of the theoretical assumptions that inform our understanding of productive early literacy environments and then reviewed the research and the tools used in the Literacy Environment Enrichment Program (LEEP). LEEP is a professional development program for early childhood educators and their supervisors promoting effective literacy and language development contexts and activities for young children. It is important to note that the supervisors were included in the professional development with the hope that they would be supportive and collaborative over time throughout the implementation of new strategies and designs for classroom contexts. The authors concluded that this intervention had been successfully maintained as a result of "deepening teachers' understanding of language and literacy and fostering more effective collaboration between teachers and supervisors . . ." (p. 198). In addition, this intervention appears to "have a dramatic positive impact on classrooms and these improvements appear to translate to better language and literacy growth." (p. 198). In other words, the essential influences on maintenance/sustainability in this case have been linked to the improved collaborative relationship between teachers and their supervisors in addition to the deep knowledge growth of the teachers. With these kinds of experiences, a teacher refines her knowledge and clarifies the rationale that is at the heart of her practice.

Finally, according to Slavin (2004), "more than 80% of all schools that implemented [the Success for All] program are still using it today" (p. 62). Success for All (SFA), the reading intervention program spearheaded by Robert Slavin, has an emphasis on prevention and early intervention for reading problems implementing strategies and instruction that are reportedly evidence based. Slavin writes that sustainability is too often difficult to support in many school change or instructional intervention programs, but SFA, because it has certain essential components, has a good record of maintenance of the program in schools that have adopted its program. The high rate of maintenance for SFA, Slavin claims, is fostered by the following essential components of the program: 1) the role of facilitators who are leaders, supporters, and collaborators; 2) the materials that are provided to the teachers as well as the school organization; 3) the required school wide commitment; 4) the consistent and reliable funding; 5) the national and local support; and 6) the continuing research and development of the program on the reading strategies and instruction.

Interestingly, the strengths of the SFA program may also be its challenges. The tight structure of the SFA program requires a strong commitment from participating teachers and an equally strong commitment from school administrators. Because of the specific requirements of the program, school administrators must be committed to creating a school culture around the program because in order for it to thrive, all classrooms must be committed to implementation of the program and its materials. To do so, it appears that all participants must believe in and be invested in the theoretical and research premises of SFA. Some may argue that the program leaves little room for creativity in teaching, but the research suggests that children do achieve with this program (Slavin & Madden, 2001 cited in Slavin, 2004). In this case, it can also be argued that sustainability of this particular reading intervention is maintained through a continued and committed collaboration among all participants.

The notion of ongoing commitment should be considered more broadly here as we think about the complexities of literacy and language learning intersecting with complexities of the development of young children. Teacher learning is also complex requiring many components to be in place. Clearly, time is a prerequisite in this commitment to learning for teachers, learning for children, and the maintenance and sustainability needed for successful outcomes.

Professional Development Activities Are Informed By Meaningful, Research-based Pedagogical Content Knowledge (PCK) (Shulman, 1987) and Best Practice

Shulman (1987) first introduced pedagogical content knowledge as being at the heart of good teaching. PCK is the intersection of knowledge of a content or discipline and knowledge of how to teach or facilitate the learning of that discipline. In the case of early language and literacy development, teachers must be knowledgeable about all aspects of research-based understandings of how young children develop language and literacy and what kinds of contexts and activities foster that development. Teachers of young children must know about oral language and its role in vocabulary development and later reading success. This knowledge must not only be research-based, but it must also make sense to practitioners as they make decisions about the instruction that will bring achievement to their students. In other words, teachers must believe that the instructional practices they are developing are rooted in substantive theory and research, will be good for their students, and will lead to measurable success for students (see Chard, 2004).

Early childhood practitioners must not only know what the essential research-based early literacy content knowledge is, they must also know how to implement the strategies, create contexts, and interact with children in ways that will promote this development. In terms of early literacy instruction for early childhood educators, a great deal of research and the literature have presented clear conclusions shared by many, of the content and process necessary for early language and literacy development of young children. In other words, there appears to be consensus across the recent early literacy literature on the content and process of fostering early literacy (Adams, 1990; Clay, 1979; Foorman & Moats, 2004; Slavin, 2004; Snow, Griffin, & Burns, 1998; Stahl & Yaden, 2004).

To begin, we have learned over time that young children's language and literacy development benefits from experiences with and contexts created by caretakers who have learned how to select books for young children, how to read aloud engagingly, how to extend the meaning of the book with additional activities, and discussions that foster oral language (vocabulary) development. Young children who have these experiences provided by knowledgeable child-care providers perform better on several early literacy behaviors such as concepts of print (Clay, 1979), writing (Purcell-Gates, 1996), and letter names (Clay, 1979) than a comparison group. (Snow, Griffin, & Burns, 1998, p. 149).

The Committee on the Prevention of Reading Difficulties in Young children (Snow, Griffin, & Burns, 1998) in their report reviewing the research on early literacy and language learning concluded that there are several areas of knowledge and experience that young children must have and the authors stressed throughout the report the importance of early childhood teachers having this knowledge of what young children need in order to become successful readers, writers, and learners. For example, the authors report that based on research and shared understanding among early literacy scholars early childhood professionals must know:

- How to provide rich conceptual experiences that promote growth in vocabulary and reasoning skills;
- Lexical development, from early referential (naming) abilities to relational and abstract terms and fine-shaped meanings;
- The early development of listening comprehension skills and the kinds of syntactic and prose structures that preschool children may not yet have mastered; young children's sense of story;
- Young children's sensitivity to the sounds of language;
- Developmental conceptions of written language (print awareness);
- Development of concepts of space, including directionality;
- Fine motor development; and
- Means for inspiring motivation to read (Snow, Griffin, & Burns, 1998, p. 280)

Similarly, Stahl and Yaden (2004) reviewed studies from the Center for Improvement of Early Reading Achievement (CIERA) that looked into several early literacy projects (Head Start, Even Start, Emergent Literacy Project, and Kindergarten Literature Program). The authors gleaned important findings across the studies. CIERA was federally funded "to generate research and create empirically based, programmatic interventions to strengthen the foundations upon which abilities in reading and writing are built" (p. 143). The authors stressed that learning to read and write involves many complex behaviors and is intricately connected to development. Stahl and Yaden present a "Developmental Theory of Learning to Read, Write, and Spell" (p. 157) informed by their review of the various CIERA studies. Essentially, children develop knowledge and understanding of the alphabetic principle as they move through phases of phonological awareness that support this growing understanding. As children advance their knowledge of how words work, they develop, for example, insights about the written word. Children begin with "the realization that spoken words can be thought of in terms of their constituent phonemes and that, in English and other alphabetic languages, letters represent these sounds" (p. 158). Young learners move through this process as they develop the insight that words contain vowels, a critical step in the knowledge of the alphabetic principle. Young children eventually develop deeper insights of the meaning of the orthography and morphology of the language.

While the authors stressed that phonological awareness is an essential understanding for the development of reading, they added that oral language development and enrichment is essential for the awareness of the phonology of the language to develop and flourish. Contexts that support rich oral language around storybook reading and first hand experiences are critical to laying the foundation for deep understanding of how language and words work (p. 147). Thus, the implications for early childhood teachers, that can be taken from the developmental theory the authors present, are that young children should have broad and varied experiences, with all forms and functions of literacy and the tools used in literate practices, while being supported by enthusiastic adults. Young children need comprehensive language experiences through first and second hand experiences and knowledge about language and its workings. Studies of the preschool and primary children's literacy learning indicates that being literate is not the acquisition of a skill, but rather it is a complex, social, long term achievement requiring thoughtful instruction, including well timed and appropriate assessment. Indeed, young children must be immersed in rich literacy and language environments.

Finally, the work of Foorman and Moats (2004) also stressed the need for teachers to be knowledgeable about research-based content and practice in order for them to authentically and successfully implement such practices. In their explanation of the professional development program conditions that were most important, the authors argued that the content knowledge presented teachers be grounded in the research. They suggested that teachers must know and understand specific topics in early literacy. Citing meta analyses in the studies of young children's necessary learning experiences in order to become successful readers (NRP, 2000; Snow et al, 1998), the authors presented the following essential early literacy topics for all teachers to build their practice around: 1) the alphabetic principle including phonemic awareness and phonics; 2) systematic phonics instruction; 3) fluency; 4) vocabulary; 5) text comprehension. This research-based content was added to pedagogical strategies in two professional development projects (District of Columbia and the Texas Initiative) promoting reading interventions. Foorman and Moats explained the important relationships among teacher knowledge, teacher competence, and classroom outcomes in their report of these initiatives and their sustainability. They concluded that the most significant obstacle to maintaining these best practices was the lack "of informed instructional leaders who can press a well-articulated initiative for several years" (p. 58), with the emphasis on "informed" and knowledgeable.

Pedagogical Content Knowledge (PCK) that is research-based and that makes good sense to practitioners is at the heart of exemplary professional development contexts. From the development of this kind of knowledge, teachers can have a solid rationale for their teaching and can create activities and contexts that promote language development through story book readings, systematic and focused experiences with phonemic awareness, first hand experiences with writing and reading for authentic purposes and immersion in a print rich, enthusiastic literature and language environment.

Professional Development Contexts Afford and Support Opportunities for Reflection and Analytical Thinking

As other learners do, teachers need opportunities to think analytically both independently and in small groups. Teachers bring their own experiences to bear on new knowledge as they reflect on, through writing and talk, all the ideas with which they are presented. Studies about and persuasive treatises on reflective teaching and the role of reflection in teacher learning dominate much of the contemporary teacher learning literature. Reflection, Dewey (Archambault, 1974) writes, affords us "intelligent action" (p. 212), providing deliberation and intentionality to what we do. He explained further that there are certain attitudes of human nature that best lend themselves to a reflective stance. *Openmindedness*, Dewey wrote, ". . . includes an active desire to listen to more sides than one; to give full attention to alternative possibilities; to recognize the possibility of error even in the beliefs that are dearest to us" (p. 224). *Wholeheartedness* arises from a deep abiding interest. "There is no greater enemy of effective thinking than divided interest" (p. 225). *Responsibility* is not only an important moral trait, Dewey explained, but being responsible intellectually ". . . means to be willing to adopt these consequences when they follow reasonably from any position already taken" (p. 226). In teaching, the process of reflection can build a bridge between theory and practice, between the technical knowledge and the craft knowledge of a discipline (Schon, 1987). Schon discerned two subtypes of reflection: reflection-in-action and reflection-on-action. The former is enacted as a teacher is managing moment-by-moment decisions and dilemmas in a classroom. It is often performed as a solo act. The latter, reflection-on-action, can be thought as reflecting at a distance from the action usually afterwards (but perhaps before as in planning) and may be enacted with others, in a dyad or small group.

Based on the work of Dewey (Archambault, 1974) and Schon (1987), Zeichner and Liston (1996) argued that reflection is the foundation not only for teacher education but continues throughout the practice of teaching. A teacher, they stressed, is responsible for her/his own professional development and the keystone of this development and growth is reflection, especially reflective teaching.

An alternative way to consider reflection as an important tool to learning and knowledge growth in teaching is the perspective of reflection as an inquiry into practice. Teachers may investigate their own practice formally or informally, with the purpose of improving upon or advancing their instructional practice. Raising questions, gathering evidence, explicating classroom dilemmas or problematizing certain student learning issues can bring about reflective inquiry, that in turn, creates the opportunity for teacher development and change, and ultimately enhances student learning.

Russell, Munby, Spafford, and Johnston (1988) argued that through the examination of one's teaching, theory is best understood as it is mapped onto practice. As problems and questions are raised through teaching practice, turning to and refining educational or pedagogical theory supports teachers as they elaborate and build on their own knowledge while constructing new knowledge as they work through practical dilemmas or are presented with new research and theory. Many scholars have written about the reliance teachers place on their experience as a way to continue learning about teaching as they "test out" new ideas (Hargreaves, 1984; Richardson, 1994; Schon, 1987; Showers, 1990).

An example of a professional development program with a high level of guidance provided by researchers/facilitators that supports teachers in reflective thinking is the Practical-Argument Staff Development Process (PASD). In The Reading Instruction Study (RIS) led by Patricia Anders and Virginia Richardson (Richardson, 1994), in-service teachers learned specific research-based reading comprehension practices within the framework of the Practical Argument activity.

The PASD researchers believed that the best way to introduce these comprehension instructional practices to teachers would be in a collaborative context, building on teachers' prior experiences and knowledge as a basis for building new understanding. Fenstermacher's (1994) conception of the process of practical argument is a means to reflect rationally on prior and future decisions. The approach involving the practical argument framework is used to guide the discourse between a teacher and researcher (or another colleague), with the purpose of analyzing instructional practice by reasoning it through and possibly, rethinking the practice. The role of the other approach was to push the teacher with questions regarding decisions, choices, judgments, and reflections. Through the practical argument process, teachers were given a structure and guided procedure for reflecting on practice, a procedure that challenged the teacher to intellectually try out alternative practices and reason through ones they were currently implementing. Gain in student achievement assessed through standardized measures was used as one indicator of the effectiveness of the PASD project.

Finally, in another example of using talk as a tool for reflection, Adger, Hoyle, and Dickinson, (2004) employed discourse analysis of dialogues conducted by teachers and facilitators during the professional development component of the Literacy Environment Enrichment Program (LEEP). LEEP is an early language and literacy intervention project developed in response to the increasing demand for knowledgeable early childhood professionals. Preschool staff members and their supervisors were enrolled in a course in which the goals were "to bring about changes in teachers' knowledge, beliefs, and practices related to literacy and to institutionalize effective practices in preschool programs" (p. 868). The authors note that comparison studies of LEEP are suggesting that the program results in "significant changes in classrooms and in children's learning" (p. 868). Grounded in sociocultural theory (see Vygotsky, 1987), Adger and associates proposed that knowledge is constructed in "professional communication" (p. 868) through discussion among participants and LEEP instructors. Indeed, these discussions provided a view into the learning that develops from participation in the LEEP course. As the researchers analyzed the discourse using the lens of sociolinguistics, they discovered specific interactions that supported a kind of "joint authorship" (p. 882) as the participants made contributions through talk, using their practical experience and new knowledge to build propositions about early language and literacy to bring to their classrooms. Evidence of the construction of joint authorship was noted as the discourse analysis showed signs indicating that the participants were interacting in an engaged manner, using behaviors such as nodding, repeating each others words and overlapping their speech (p. 882).

These instructional conversations provided a "fertile ground for learning" (p. 894) and evidence of new knowledge construction as the discourse mediated the developing understandings. Interestingly, an idea central to the LEEP course is that the development of oral language is the underpinning for children's literacy development. Teachers are thus encouraged to design contexts that present activities rich with opportunities for children to talk together, and with, their teachers. In order to model these activities, the course itself provides occasions for participants to talk and collaborate through discussion. In their analyses of the teacher/participant discourse, the researchers found evidence that new, research-based knowledge was being linked to practical knowledge and that these discursive interactions supported reflection and elaboration of learning. Finally, the authors suggest that this kind of participation in "jointly authored discourse" (p. 895) may foster the ability to build the same kinds of conversations with children as well as with colleagues. However, we argue that as a tool for reflection and learning these professional discussions linking practical experiences with theory and research suggest a powerful activity for knowledge construction and advancing understanding and commitment. Experiences promoting reflection and analytical thinking, while connecting theory and practice, are the cornerstone for professional development programs.

In the next section we review two programs of research in early literacy and language professional development, CIERA and LEEP. Connections are made between professional development research literature viewed broadly and viewed specifically for early childhood teachers.

Best practices in Early Language and Literacy Professional Development Programs: Incorporating the Four Features

In this section we discuss two early literacy intervention/research programs, CIERA and LEEP. In both projects, in-service teacher learning was a critical component of the work. In both projects, best practices for professional development were implemented as well as investigated. Each early literacy program adds to the literature on the effective features of professional development contexts that foster sustainable teacher learning.

The Center for the Improvement of Early Reading Achievement (CIERA)

CIERA, a comprehensive five year research and intervention program was sponsored by the Office of Educational Research from 1997-2002. Its conceptual goals included a study of the early reading processes while addressing reading problems, instruction, and the influence of context on reading success. In addition, the CIERA researchers aimed at bringing the research on early reading to teachers, parents, and administrators as well as to educational researchers. Arriving at a time when instruction, especially literacy instruction, was being driven more forcefully by federal and state standards, CIERA researchers took on the responsibility of: 1) identifying research-based instructional programs in schools; 2) investigating the effects of inclusion of students with disabilities as well as cultural and linguistic diversity; 3) understanding effective teacher education and professional development in literacy; and 4) including state and federal standards and accountability (Carlisle & Hiebert, 2004).

CIERA's program of research included three lines of inquiry: 1) Readers and text; 2) Home and school; and 3) Policy and profession. The research took various theoretical and methodological approaches and worked toward both breadth and depth in the varied approaches and perspectives taken by the researchers (see www.ciera.org). Contributions to research from the many studies spanning the five year period are multifaceted and enlightening. For example, much has been learned about the important characteristics that influence success in literacy development in kindergarten. From the CIERA project we have learned about the critical role of texts and children's reading achievement as well as the influence of policy on state standards regarding literacy instruction and assessment and the need to match curriculum goals with instruction and assessment. Finally, and important to our purposes in this chapter, the work from CIERA researchers has offered important understandings about the power of professional development in early literacy instruction as part of change or intervention. While many of the CIERA studies included a description and evaluation of professional development contexts linked to it (Taylor & Pearson, 2004), other studies focused only on the programs for professional development and looked at the use of technology to foster collaboration and reflection as well as the relationship between facilitators and teachers and collaboration as features of professional development activities (Carlisle & Hiebert, 2004; La Fevre & Richardson, 2002; Wixson & Yocum, 2004; Zhao & Rop, 2001).

Taylor and Pearson (2004) reviewed the CIERA studies that reflect successful school change as a result of the connections across school, home and the community. They argued that for school change to be successful, especially in early literacy instruction intervention, teachers must be provided with the "best research on reading instruction available," (p. 178) and that change follows when there is strong "teacher involvement and ownership over the change process" (p. 178). In fact, the authors explain that it is through "collaborative, ongoing professional development" that teachers "improve their capacity to teach reading to children in high-poverty schools" (p. 178). In other words, Taylor and Pearson found what other researchers have also found; teacher learning is at the heart of successful school improvement, and teachers need structure and support for professional development in order to take the ownership necessary to implement the best practices to foster early literacy learning, and to collaborate with others while reflecting on their teaching.

As discussed earlier in this chapter and as part of the larger CIERA study investigating what kinds of literacy interventions are successful, La Fevre and

Richardson (2002) examined the qualities and dilemmas of the roles and relationships of the professional development facilitators (or staff developers) and participating teachers by surveying facilitators across three professional development contexts for literacy intervention and instructional change. The researchers asked two questions: 1) What do facilitators do in successful programs of literacy intervention? and 2) How can successful professional development be described? Each context had very different design characteristics presenting both opportunities and challenges to all participants. The facilitators interviewed for this paper were staff developers for Success for All (focus on skills for success for students in reading in low SES schools); Reading Recovery (intensive one-to-one program based on the work of Marie Clay (1979); The Literacy Program (balanced literacy and supports for district wide change); The Eclectic School Program (using a variety of programs over time); or the State Standards Project (collaboration between state department of education and university involves teachers in designing effective instruction). The programs were placed on a continuum from externally developed or highly scripted (Success for All and Reading Recovery) to less externally developed or Adaptation of External Programs (Eclectic Program and the Literacy Program) to Internally Developed New Programs (the State Standards Program). The researchers learned that the stance taken by the facilitators, that is, how they perceived their roles and their beliefs about the program itself, was dependent upon whether the program was externally or internally driven. LaFevre and Richardson explained the relationship between the facilitator and the context or program in this way: Success for All is externally developed/scripted and so, the facilitator's stance is one of Direct Instruction. Reading Recovery is also externally developed, however, the facilitator in this program took a Direct/Dialogical stance. The Literacy program and the Eclectic Program were both externally developed/adapted. The facilitators in these contexts took a Direct Dialogical stance. The State standards project was internally developed and the facilitator's stance was collaborative. Thus, the facilitators' approaches to their roles and relationships were dependent on the conceptual and instructional framework of the various programs (p. 498).

In addition, there were common beliefs across the facilitators as to the characteristics of successful professional development programs. They agreed on the need for a sense of community and trust and the support of the larger community such as the school itself. In addition, there were dilemmas the facilitators noted in common such as trying to build trust while advancing the learning in a challenging manner. They also noted the dilemma of allowing for a balance of individual autonomy and externally driven agendas. Indeed, questions were raised about who sets the agenda or who determines the direction of the work. Collegiality and collaboration emerge here as important and complex issues.

In an effort to examine how technology may support both reflection and collegiality in professional development, Zhao and Rop (2001), as part of Inquiry 3 of the CIERA project, reviewed all the published literature regarding electronic networks or Computer Mediated Communication (CMC) as a site for community and reflective discourse. They found that while the interest was there for the use of technology for teachers to learn and talk together, there was not sufficient rigorous research to tell us much about the quality of the reflective discourse or the community using CMC. The authors reported that the CMC networks they studied fell into three types: networks that shared information, fostered professional development, and created communities (p. 4). However, since the papers reporting on these networks did not clearly define community or reflection, it was difficult to measure if a community had been formed, if reflective discourse was ongoing, and if indeed, there was evidence of teacher learning throughout these engagements. In addition, however, Zhao and Rop learned from this review that these communication networks appeared to be somewhat successful and they proposed the following factors essential (but not enough) to get teachers to talk with each other: 1) Technology—it had to work well and seamlessly; 2) Motivation—the teachers had to have something to talk about that was of interest to them, not necessarily what the university researchers implementing the network wanted them to discuss; 3) Time frame of the project—it often was not long enough to support sustainability; 4) Time to participate—teachers had to find the time to spend online with the network; 5) Project goals—the goals should be adjusted to show evidence of reflective discourse and community development as well as provide novel ways to consider the outcomes of the activity). In other words, while the expectations have been high for CMC, very little is understood about its effectiveness (pp. 8–9).

As part of the CIERA third Inquiry strand targeting policy and professional development implications of early literacy interventions, Wixson and Yocum (2004) examined the impact of state standards for literacy instruction on teaching, teachers, and professional development. In reviewing several CIERA professional development projects, they concluded that collaboration and learning that developed in teacher communities of practice contributed to teacher learning and improvement in students' reading achievement (for example, Florio-Ruane & Raphael, 2001). Teacher communities of practice are collaborative groups of teachers who come together to inquire into their practice with the goal of advancing their knowledge about specific teaching practices and understandings (see Palincsar, et al, 1998). These communities are often powerful contexts for learning and inquiry as teachers construct new advanced understandings grounded in their experience, their practice, and their expertise. In this process teachers, through inquiry and discussion, investigate teaching dilemmas, and decisions related to student learning. In addition, Wixson and Yocum explained that communities of practice in the CIERA studies were most successful when they were connected by "strong, centralized supports and networks or . . . include[d] strong teacher leaders." (p. 239)

The work of Susan Florio-Ruane and Taffy Raphael has provided additional studies supported by CIERA. Over the last few years these scholars have been deeply interested in fostering teachers' learning in literacy instruction by offering contexts and activities in which teachers are researchers and inquirers (Florio-Ruane & Raphael, 2000; Raphael, Forio-Ruane, Kehus, George, Hasty, & Highfield, 2000). "Teacher inquiry networks," were first initiated in the experience of book club discussion groups (Raphael, Florio-Ruane, Kehus, George, Hasty, & Highfield, 2000) and using literature discussion as the activity (Literary Circle), the teachers and researchers have moved teacher research into best practices in literacy instruction. From the Literary Circle experience the inquiry network made up of teacher study groups emerged. The Teachers' Learning Collaborative (TLC) is a network of study groups comprised of teachers. In these study groups teachers take on many of the complex issues and problems of bringing rich, literature based literacy experiences to their students in the classroom. Specifically, the overarching question was "How can we re-engage low-achieving readers?" (Raphael et al, p. 2). Through inquiry into their classrooms and collaborative curriculum design, the teacher participants created and implemented meaningful, research-based literacy curriculum that engages all learners, while grounded in literature and classroom discourse. While the TLC has professional connections with university teacher educators and researchers, the work of these communities of practice is teacher driven as the teachers raise instructional problems linked to practice.

Virginia Richardson, in association with Barbara Taylor and David Pearson, have conducted research as part of the Instructional Change Study, a CIERA project at the University of Michigan (Richardson, 2001) which has developed a set of critical characteristics for teacher change. These recommended characteristics come from their research, the literature, and Richardson's longstanding work (Richardson, 1994) on factors that promote change in teachers' thinking and thus, learning. Richardson explained that for change to evolve at the school level, the several components must be in place. Using their combined expertise, Richardson, in collaboration with Taylor and Pearson, proposed that the following characteristics be present in the introduction of a school wide reading program intervention:

a) A majority of teachers (75%) in the school must participate in the program. b) A knowledgeable facilitator supports teachers in the process. c) There is a team leading the change that includes representatives from each grade level appointed by the principal or chosen by the teachers. d) Most of the planning is developed at grade level meetings where teachers, while provided with experts to help and with choices of research-based programs, make decisions about changes in instructional programs. e) The project is always informed by the information taken from student test scores and classroom observations (pp. 7–8).

Finally, in an interesting study of researcher and teacher collaboration as a form of professional development, Yaden and Tam (2000) reported on the dilemmas connected to top down presentations of research-based instructional interventions to a teacher who has not quite bought into the technique. In their paper, the authors describe the negotiations conducted as researchers and teachers made sense of an early literacy intervention technique. The work was done in a bilingual childcare center in downtown Los Angeles. The center was located in a high poverty neighborhood. The researchers attempted to introduce the teacher to the use of a big book in the shared reading activity in order for him to support the children in learning about concepts about print. The teacher, as reported by Yaden and Tam, was a gifted story teller and preferred to use his unique narrative style to tell the story while holding the book but not making the parts of the book especially explicit. The teacher resisted the use of the big book until a solution was reached. The children and the teacher would write their own big book together, and in doing so, concepts about print would be addressed. In this case, the teacher understood and accepted the rationale for the use of big books, however, he was unable to implement shared reading and big books in the way that the researchers asked him to. The teacher, using his skills, knowledge, and expertise, was able to implement the new instructional intervention that was meaningful and appropriate for him and for his students, an intriguing example of collaboration, negotiation and inquiry.

In conclusion, the rich, complex, and varied work from the Center for the Improvement of Early Reading Achievement (CIERA) has contributed a great deal to the professional development literature and to our thinking about the best practices for creating effective contexts for teacher learning about early literacy and language.

The Literacy Environment and Enrichment Program

After studying the nature and quality of contexts for language and literacy development in pre schools, especially those that serve children who come from families with low SES and finding that many caregivers do not have the knowledge about emergent literacy practices, the Educational Development Center's (EDC) Center for Children and Families created a program for the professional development of teachers of very young children (Dickinson & Sprague, 2002). Developing from a teacher-researcher collaboration at a Head Start center, the Literacy Environment and Enrichment Program was a professional development project meant for early childhood caregivers to support them in their developing understanding of research-based practices to foster language and literacy development in young children by providing enriched contexts in preschool settings. The goal for the LEEP program was to provide professionals with the pedagogical content knowledge (Shulman, 1987) necessary to foster the development of language and literacy in young children (Dickinson & Brady, 2006). The course of study provided in the LEEP program was college credit bearing and centered around four aspects: 1) knowledge of literacy and language development; 2) knowledge of the ways in which informal assessment can be implemented and used to inform practice; 3) knowledge about teaching and organizational strategies for literacy and language; 4) guidance of teachers in the use of reflection to deepen their new understandings (p. 148).

Studies of these early LEEP classrooms—those contexts where teachers participated in the LEEP courses and gained knowledge and experiences with the above 4 components—indicate that children were "rated significantly higher in the fall than in the spring on reading and writing. In addition, teachers rated children as displaying fewer problem behaviors, possibly suggesting that, as the classroom curriculum becomes more lively, children become more engaged and less likely to amuse themselves in inappropriate ways . . . these results indicate that LEEP has a positive effect on teachers and that children benefit from the changes teachers have implemented." (Dickinson & Sprague, 2002, p. 275)

The Literacy Environment and Enrichment Program continued to evolve over time including various iterations such as T-LEEP, STARS/LEEP, PD-LIT. Dickinson and Brady (2006) present important lessons learned and recommendations gleaned from experiences in each of these studies. Two areas concerned with the outcomes of the intervention were the process and the content. The process of the professional development included issues such as time, the manner in which the content was presented and organized, and the support provided for participating teachers. The researchers found that the timing of the course work had to be carefully considered. For example, teachers needed time to think about the substance of the ideas and time for trying out new ideas in their classrooms and then reflecting on their observations.

So, the conceptual breadth and depth of the material presented may influence the frequency of the teaching sessions and the extent over time of the sessions. Also, as LEEP evolved the amount and quality of support for the teachers in the classroom also evolved and increased as researchers learned that support from supervisors played a key role.

Researchers learned from these studies that the organization and presentation of the content of the course work were critical to the effectiveness of teachers' learning and implementation of best practice. Across all of the LEEP iterations, the researchers implemented techniques to foster reflection and collaborative problem solving. The credit bearing course work associated with LEEP afforded the richest opportunities for practicing reflection as the teachers were required to reflect on their attempts to match their learning with their classroom practice and reflect on those observations as part of the course requirements. The joint problem solving emerged through the practice of class discussions during the LEEP classes as teachers discussed topics presented with the use of videos or work samples. In these discussions, teachers would call upon their own experiences in their classrooms to contribute ideas to these discussions (Adger et al, 2004) Every day the LEEP teachers were immersed in practice and so were in the position to try out their new learning, observe what happened, and reflect upon those observations—matching theory to practice. An important influence on the effectiveness of the teacher learning outcomes was the attrition rate. The researchers learned that motivating early childhood care providers to participate in professional development programs is essential and indeed, often a challenge. The critical influences on the rate of attrition noted here are: "academic preparation of the teachers, teachers' expectations of the experience, on-site support for academic challenges, the nature of extrinsic motivators and the teacher's intrinsic motivation, life circumstances, and program support" (p. 164). Time requirements in the program may also be strongly influential on the willingness of teachers to participate and stay involved. The data suggested that courses that required more class sessions with shorter time between class meetings had a higher rate of attrition.

The lessons learned from all versions of LEEP have set the groundwork for planning the scaling up or institutionalization of such professional development programs for early childhood educators. The results from the PD-LIT version in particular indicate that on-site support provided through well trained mentors who are part of the center staff is worth careful consideration. Thus, building on the professional relationships already established, the professional development, and the ongoing learning of all staff, becomes integral to the culture of the school community.

REFERENCES

Adams, M. J. (1990). *Beginning to read.* Cambridge, MA: The MIT Press.

Adger, C. T., Hoyle, S. M., & Dickinson, D. K. (2004). Locating learning in the in-service education for preschool teachers. *American Educational Research Journal, 41*(4), 867-900.

Archambault, R. D. (Ed.) (1974). *John Dewey on education.* Chicago: The University of Chicago Press.

Birman, B. F., Desimone, L., Porter, A. C., & Garet, M. S. (2000). Designing professional development that works. *Educational Leadership, 57*(8), 28-33.

Carlisle, J. F. & Hiebert, E. (2004). Introduction: The context and contributions of research at the Center for the Improvement of Early Reading Achievement. *The Elementary School Journal, 105*(2), 131-139.

Chard, D. J. (2004). Towards a science of professional development in early reading instruction. *Exceptionality, 12*(3), 175-191.

Clay, M. M. (1979). *The early detection of reading difficulties.* Auckland, NZ: Heinemann.

Cochran-Smith, M. & Lytle, S. (1992). Communities for teacher research: Fringe or forefront? *American Journal of Education,* 298-324.

Cochran-Smith, M. & Lytle, S. (1999). The teacher research movement: A decade later. *Educational Researcher, 28*(7), 15-25.

Cohen, D. & Ball, D. (1990). Policy and practice: An overview. *Educational Evaluation and Policy Analysis, 12*(3), 233-239.

Darling-Hammond, L. (1990). Instructional policy into practice: The power of the bottom over the top. *Educational Evaluation and Policy analysis, 12*(3), 339-347.

Dickinson, D. & Brady, J. P. (2006). Toward effective support for language and literacy through professional development. In Zaslow, M. & Martinez-Beck, I. (Eds.) *Critical issues in early childhood professional development* (pp. 141-170). Baltimore: Paul H. Brookes, Publishing Co.

Dickinson, D. & Sprague, K. E. (2002). The nature and impact of early childhood care environments on the language and early literacy development of children from low-income families. In Neuman, S.B & Dickinson, D.K. (Eds.) *Handbook of early literacy research* (pp. 281-292). New York: The Guilford Press.

Dickinson, & McCabe (2001). Bringing it all together: The multiple origins, skills and environmental supports of early literacies. *Learning Disabilities Research & Practice, 16*(4), 186-202.

Fenstermacher, G. D. (1994). The place of practical argument in the education of teachers. In V. Richardson (Ed.). *Teacher change and the staff development process* (pp. 23-42). New York: Teachers College Press.

Florio-Ruane & Raphael, T. E. (2000). Reading lives: Creating and sustaining learning about culture and literacy education in teacher study groups. Archive article #00-08. Retrieved 3/27/06 from http://www.ciera.org.

Foorman, B. R. & Moats, L. C. (2004). Conditions for sustaining research-based practice in early reading instruction. *Remedial and Special Education, 25*(1), 51-60.

Fullan, M. (1991). *The new meaning of educational change*. Second edition. New York: Teachers College Press.

Grimmet, P. P. & Crehan, E. P. (1992). The nature of collegiality in teacher development: The case of clinical supervision. In M. Fullan & A. Hargreaves (Eds.) *Teacher development and educational change* (pp. 56–85). London: The Falmer Press.

Grossman, P. L. (1992). Changing roles and relationships of teachers as learners and leaders. In A. Lieberman (Ed.) *The changing contexts of teaching*. Ninety-first yearbook of the National Society for the Study of Education. Part 1. (pp. 179–196). Chicago: The University of Chicago Press.

Guskey, T. (1986). Staff development and the process of teacher change. *Educational Researcher, 15*(5), 5–15.

Hargreaves, A. (1996). *Changing teachers, changing times: Teachers' work and culture in the postmodern age*. New York: Teachers College Press.

Hawley, W. D. & Valli, L. (1999). The essentials of effective professional development: A new consensus. In L. Darling-Hammond & G. Sykes (Eds.), *Teaching as the learning profession: A handbook of policy and practice* (pp. 127-150). San Francisco: Jossey-Bass.

LaFevre D. & Richardson, V. (2002). Staff development in early reading intervention programs: The facilitator. *Teaching and Teacher Education, 18*, 483–500.

Leont'ev, A. N. (1979). The problem of activity in psychology. In J.V. Wertsch (Ed.), *The concept of activity in soviet psychology* (pp. 37-71). Armonk, NY: M.E. Sharpe, Inc.

Little, J. W. (1992). Opening the black box of professional community. In A. Leiberman (Ed.), *The changing context of teaching* (pp. 157-178). Chicago: The University of Chicago Press.

Little, J. W. (1999). Organizing schools for teacher learning. In L. Darling-Hammond & G. Sykes (Eds.), *Teaching as the learning profession: A handbook of policy and practice* (pp. 233–262). San Francisco: Jossey-Bass.

Little, J. W. (1990). The persistence of privacy: Autonomy and initiative in teachers' professional relations. *Teachers College Record, 91*, 509–536.

Little, J. W. & McLaughlin, M. W. (1993). (Eds.) *Teachers' work: Individuals, colleagues, and contexts*. New York: Teachers College Press.

Lortie, D. C. (1975). *Schoolteacher*. Chicago: The University of Chicago Press.

National Association for the Education of Young Children. (1998). Learning to read and write: Developmentally appropriate practices for young children. Joint position statement of the International Reading Association (IRA) and *the National Association for the Education of Young Children (NAEYC), 53(4)*.

National Reading Panel (2000). *Teaching children to read*. Jessup, MD: Education Publications Center.

No Child Left Behind Act of 2001. Retrieved on April 6, 2006 from, www.ed.gov/policy/elsec/leg/esea02/107-110.pdf.

Palincsar, A. S., Magnusson, S. J., Marano, N., Ford, D., & Brown, N. (1998). Designing a community of practice: Principles and practices of the GIsML community. *Teaching and Teacher Education, 14*(1), 5–19.

Purcell-Gates, V. (1996). Stories, coupons, and the TV guide: Relationships between home literacy experiences and emergent literacy knowledge. *Reading Research Quarterly, 31,* 406–428.

Raphael, T. E., Florio-Ruane, S., Kehus, M., George, M., Hasty, N. & Highfield, K. (2000). Thinking for ourselves: Literacy learning in a diverse teacher inquiry network, Archive article #00-07. Retrieved on March 27, 2006 from, http://www.ciera.org.

Richardson, V. (1994). (Ed.) *Teacher change and the staff development process: A case in reading instruction.* New York: Teachers College Press.

Richardson, V. (2001). Alexis de Toqueville and the dilemmas of professional development. Retrieved on March 23, 2006 from, http://www. ciera.org/library/archive/2001-12/22oct01-104-MS_POST.htm

Rogoff, B. (1990). *Apprenticeship in thinking.* New York: Oxford University Press.

Russell, T., Munby, H., Spafford, C. & Johnston, P. (1988). Learning the professional knowledge of teaching: Metaphors, puzzles, and the theory-practice relationship. In P. Grimmet & G. Erickson (Eds.), *Reflection in teacher education* (pp. 67–89). New York: Teachers College Press.

Schon, D. A. (1987). *Educating the reflective practitioner: Toward a new design for teaching and learning in the professions.* San Francisco: Jossey-Bass.

Showers, B. (1990). Aiming for superior classroom instruction for all children: A comprehensive staff development model. *Remedial and Special Education, 11*(3), 35–39.

Slavin, R. (2004). Built to last: Long term maintenance of Success for All. *Remedial and Special Education, 25*(1), 61–66.

Shulman, L. S. (1987). Knowledge and teaching: Foundations of the new reform. *Harvard Educational Review, 57*(1), 1–22.

Snow, C. E., Burns, M. S., & Griffin, P.(1998) (Eds) *Preventing reading difficulties in young children.* Washington, DC: National Academy Press.

Stahl, S. A. & Yaden, D. B. (2004). The development of literacy in preschool and primary grades: Work by the Center for the Improvement of Early Reading Achievement. *The Elementary School Journal, 105*(2), 141–165.

Strickland, D. S. & Barnett, W. S. (2003). Literacy interventions for preschool children considered at risk: Implications for curriculum, professional development, and parent involvement. *National Reading Conference Yearbook, 52,* 104–116.

Sykes, G. (1999). Teacher and student learning: Strengthening their connection. In L. Darling-Hammond & G. Sykes (Eds.), *Teaching as the learning profession: A handbook of policy and practice* (pp. 151–179). San Francisco: Jossey-Bass.

Taylor, B. M. & Pearson, P. D. (2004). Research on learning to read—at school, at home, and in the community. *The Elementary School Journal, 105*(2), 167–188.

Vygotsky, L. S. (1987). The collected works of L. S. Vygotsky: Volume I problems of general psychology. New York: Plenum.

Wertsch, J. V. (1998). *Mind as action.* New York: Oxford University Press.

Wixson, K. K. & Yochum, N. (2004). Research on literacy policy and professional development: National, state, district, and teacher contexts. *The Elementary School Journal, 105*(2), 219–242.

Yaden, D. B. & Tam, A. (2000). Enhancing emergent literacy in a preschool program through teacher-researcher collaboration. CIERA Report #2-011. Retrieved on March 23, 2006 from, http://www.ciera.org.

Zeichner, K. M. & Liston, D. P. (1996). *Reflective teaching: An introduction.* Mahwah, NJ: Lawrence Erlbaum Associates.

Zhao, Y. & Rop, S. A critical review of the literature on electronic networks as reflective discourse communities for in-service teachers. Retrieved on March 2, 2006 from, http://www.ciera.org/library/reports/inquiry-3/3-014/3-014.htm

Chapter Six

Evaluation Study of Striving to Achieve Reading Success Project STARS

Norris M. Haynes
with Michael Ben-Avie, Joy Fopiano, Maureen Gilbride-Redman, Susan Tiso, Nnandi Ihuegbu

INTRODUCTION

Early Reading Success

In 1998–99, extending the work already begun for preschool youngsters, the Connecticut State Assembly enacted Public Act 99-227, which provided for a statewide Early Reading Success Institute (ERSI). The Institute was accompanied by the formation of an Early Reading Success Panel whose mission included assessing reading instruction needs of priority school districts and creating a professional development plan for these districts (Connecticut State Department of Education, 2000). *Connecticut's Blueprint for Reading Achievement* contained the results of the panel's study and its recommendations, including explanations of the importance of oral language as a foundation for reading, and a detailed guide for a comprehensive reading instruction program. In addition, the *Blueprint* outlined the necessary literacy competencies for teachers and learners for each grade level, Kindergarten through Grade Three. The ERSI was enacted for the dissemination of the Blueprint's findings among teachers in Connecticut. The primary mission of the Institute was to support teachers in learning about the *Blueprint* and its research premise, and to acquire the knowledge base necessary for designing learning contexts that foster comprehensive reading instruction. The Institute collaborated with the Connecticut State Department of Education, members of the Regional Education Service Centers, district literacy coordinators, school principals, and other staff, including K-3 classroom teachers. As a result of this professional development program, teachers would have a useful guide to learner competencies for literacy at all the primary levels, as well as a framework of knowledge to plan meaningful instruction.

While *Connecticut's Blueprint for Reading Achievement* represents a comprehensive research-based explanation and description of reading instruction in the primary grades, it also points to the preschool years as the optimal time for establishing oral language development as a foundation for emergent literacy. Literacy-rich learning centers promote and enhance phonological sensitivity and thus, phoneme awareness, and in turn, support the developing knowledge and use of meaningful vocabulary (Watson, 2002; Dickinson & Sprague, 2002). The report from The Early Reading Success Panel in directing the work of the primary grades made salient two additional requirements: (1) the design and construction of learning contexts that foster literacy and language development for young children; and (2) a provision for professional development for early childhood educators and caregivers to learn about the importance of these contexts and ways to create them.

PROJECT STARS: THREE STRATEGIES

The First Strategy: Literacy Environment Enrichment Program (LEEP)

Literacy Environment Enrichment Program is a professional development program designed by researchers and practitioners at EDC's Center for Children and Families for early childhood teachers and their supervisors. Developed with funding from the U.S. Department of Health and Human Services, the U.S. Department of Education, and the Spencer Foundation, LEEP is based on research regarding children's language development, early literacy learning, and effective models of supervision.

The LEEP course, as offered by Project STARS, is a four-credit college level course with both a graduate and undergraduate credit option available to students. Through Project STARS, credit is offered for the LEEP course through both Southern Connecticut State University and The University of Connecticut. Students sign up for and attend the course in teams of two or three, consisting of one or two preschool teachers and a center supervisor. While teachers and supervisors cover much of the same literacy-related content, LEEP sessions periodically divide participants into affinity groups so that teachers can delve more deeply into classroom practice and supervisors can learn specific strategies to support teachers' adoption of new practices. Assignments, which are performance-based, are differentiated along the same lines. LEEP's face-to-face sessions are supplemented by supervisor cluster meetings and individual on-site support provided by instructors. The course is taught by teams consisting of EDC LEEP instructors and professors from higher education institutions in Connecticut. There are three instructors who each teach the teams of supervisor/preschool teachers. One of the instructors is dedicated to supervisors.

The Second Strategy: Connecticut Charts-A-Course's New Literacy Strand

Another strategy for Project STARS, is the development and implementation of a revised literacy "strand" of Connecticut Charts-A-Course (CCAC). A strand is a curricular unit. Supported by Connecticut legislators and early childhood and school age educators, the CCAC network was first introduced in 1991. CCAC collaborates with the Connecticut State Department of Education, the Department of Social Services, and Connecticut Community Colleges. The early childhood education curriculum supports a developmental progression for the careers of early childhood professionals who are preparing for their Child Development Associate (CDA). The curriculum includes eight core areas of knowledge for teachers of young children: 1) providing a safe, healthy and purposeful learning environment; 2) learning about child growth and development; 3) advancing children's physical and intellectual development; 4) advancing children's social and emotional development; 5) managing an effective program; 6) establishing productive relationships with families; 7) assessing children's learning and development; and 8) advancing professionalism. Under the auspices of Project STARS, CCAC and EDC analyzed the current literacy modules, and with other literacy advisors made recommendations for revisions. CCAC then created and implemented a curricular literacy strand for pre-CDA educators that is consistent with the research base of LEEP.

The Third Strategy: Higher Education Faculty Institute

As the third strategy of Project STARS, The Special Education Resource Center (SERC) coordinates institutes for professors of preservice teachers. Bearing in mind the overall goal to help children from priority districts become successful academically, the institute provides faculty in higher education with the current research in literacy and language development in young children. The intent is that teacher educators will, in turn, contribute to advancing the knowledge base for both preservice and in-service teachers and administrators in their college and university classrooms and in workshops. The institutes have included presentations given by national experts in literacy for faculty from various independent and public colleges and universities in Connecticut.

METHODOLOGY

Study Participants

Adult Samples

The first study sample consisted of adult participants in EDC's Literacy Environment Enrichment Program (LEEP). Within this study sample, there were two subgroups: supervisors and teachers.The second study sample consisted of instructors of the LEEP program. There were three instructors per site. A total of eight sites were observed over two years. These instructors were evaluated as part of CCSAR's evaluation of the LEEP training sessions. The third study sample consisted of participants in the Connecticut Charts-A-Course (CCAC) training program. This population was composed of any preschool provider, regardless of their role (i.e., supervisor, assistant), who participated in the CCAC Literacy Strand.The fourth study sample was the Comparison group. This group consisted of supervisors and teachers of preschools that were not currently enrolled in either LEEP or the Literacy Strand of CCAC.The fifth study sample consisted of participants in the Higher Education Faculty Institute that was organized by the Special Education Research Center. Participants in this institute included faculty from 2- and 4-year colleges. The sixth study sample consisted of participants in five focus group interviews. Two groups consisted of supervisors and teachers who attended the LEEP training; two groups consisted of members from the State Department of Education who directed Project STARS; and one group consisted of members of EDC who had developed the LEEP training, and the instructors of the LEEP training.

Children Samples

The first study sample consisted of children who attended preschools that sent supervisors and teachers to LEEP training.The second study sample consisted of children who attended preschools that were not affiliated with LEEP or CCAC Literacy Strand training.

Description of Research Instruments

Children Outcome Measures

Peabody Picture Vocabulary Test (PPVT). The *PPVT*, developed by L. M. Dunn and I. M. Dunn (1981), is used (1) to assess receptive language, vocabulary and verbal intelligence; and (2) to screen for learning and linguistic problems. The test purports to provide a nonverbal estimate of verbal intelligence (Kaplan & Saccuzzo, 2001., p. 325) for children ages two and a half through eighteen years. Study subjects are asked to look at a picture card that shows four pictures. While looking at the picture cards, the subjects hear a word spoken by the examiner. The subjects are asked to indicate which of the four pictures most closely matches the spoken word. The picture cards are ordered in increasing level of difficulty. There are 175 picture cards for each of two forms. These two forms may be used to administer a pre-test and a post-test. The total score can be converted to a standard score, percentile rank, stanine or age-equivalent score. Administration of the *PPVT* takes about 15 minutes.

Modified-Profile of Early Literacy Development (Modified-PELD). The *Profile of Early Literacy Development (PELD)* was developed by Dickinson and Chaney (1997). *PELD* is a direct measure of literacy and phonemic awareness among preschool children. EDC revised the *PELD* in 2001 and created the *Assessment of Early Literacy and Language Development (AELLD)*. The intent of the revision was to develop an instrument that was appropriate not only for preschool children, but also for children in kindergarten. The Center for Community and School Action Research's (CCSAR's) faculty felt that the *AELLD* could be made more effective for preschool children.Therefore, for the purpose of this study (and with EDC's permission), CCSAR designed a modified version of the *PELD*, *Modified-PELD*. CCSAR matched sections of the *PELD* with similar sections in the *AELLD*. The following are the subscales of the *Modified-PELD*: Phoneme Deletion, Rhyme Recognition, Rhyme Production, Reading Environmental Print, Sense of Printed Language, Print Concepts (Part I), Print Concepts (Part II), Listening Comprehension, Letter Identification, Name Writing, and Sentence Dictation. Administration of the *Modified-PELD*. It takes about 25 to 30 minutes.

Adult Beliefs, Practices and Attitude Measures

The Literacy, Language and Curriculum Belief and Practices of Preschool Teachers ("Beliefs"). The *"Beliefs"* is a 60-item questionnaire that is aligned with the goals and objectives of EDC's LEEP course. Developed by David Dickinson at EDC, it is a self-report survey administered to teachers and supervisors in early childhood centers. It measures participants' knowledge and understanding of research-based early language and literacy development. It also collects self-report data from teachers on their use of effective teaching practices with children and their involvement with families. Psychometric data for the instrument is not yet available but is being developed. The instrument has a 40- to 50-minute completion time.

Supervisory Practices and Attitudes (SPA). *SPA* is a questionnaire completed by supervisors in early childhood centers. Developed by EDC's Dickinson and Chalufour in 2001, it seeks supervisors' evaluation of staffs' performance in the classroom. It also obtains information on supervisors' hiring practices and criteria for staff evaluation. The questionnaire has a 20- to 30-minute completion time.

Adult Roles in the Classroom (ARIC). ARIC (Dickinson, 1999) seeks information on how teachers and assistant teachers in early childhood centers use their time during students' meal times and free play. The observation is conducted by an evaluator who checks all items that apply to the teacher's behavior in the classroom. There are 15 items on the instrument, including possible positive and negative behaviors of the teachers. ARIC has a completion time of 30 minutes.

Classroom Environment Measure

Early Language and Literacy Classroom Observation (ELLCO). To determine the nature and quality of preschool classrooms' environmental support for children's emerging literacy, evaluators complete the *ELLCO* (Smith, Dickinson and Sangeorge, 2001) when observing classrooms. The *ELLCO* Toolkit consists of three parts: a Literacy Environment Checklist, a Classroom Observation form, and the Literacy Activities Rating Scale. For the purposes of ranking classrooms (i.e., weak, basic, and strong), only the Classroom Observation component is used. Generally observations are completed within three hours.

Other Measures

Literacy Training Index (LTI). The *LTI* (Dickinson, 2001) measures the quality of the training that is provided under the auspices of Project STARS. *LTI* is a 14-item questionnaire that was administered to LEEP participants at the end of training. It has a completion time of 15 to 30 minutes.

Higher Education Faculty Institute Survey

The Higher Education Faculty Institute Survey was composed by CCSAR, SERC, and CCAC (2002). Section one requests demographic information from the participants. Sections two focuses on content acquisition in early language and literacy. Section three focuses on the targeted content or skills in course syllabi.

Samples and Instruments

Table 6.1 is a summary of the sample. It identifies which instruments were used with each population. In the table, Y1 refers to Year One and Y2 refers to Year Two.

Table 6.1. Samples and Instruments

Evaluations		Number of Evaluations Collected				Total Pre Evaluations for Study Sample (Y1 & Y2)	Total Post for Study Sample (Y1 & Y2)
Sample	Instrument	Year One Pre	Year One Post	Year Two Pre	Year Two Post		
LEEP	PPVT	42	29	15	15	57	44
	PELD	41	29	14	14	55	43
	ELLCO	15	14	18	18	33	32
	ARIC	15	15	18	18	33	33
	"Beliefs"	54	30	73	69	127	99
	SPA	17	9	23	20	40	29
LEEP Instructors	Lit. Training Index		72		80		152
Comparison	PPVT	25	13	16	11	41	24
	PELD	25	13	16	10	41	23
	ELLCO	20	15	21	20	41	35
	ARIC	20	14	21	20	41	34
	"Beliefs"	135	16	46	18	181	34
	SPA	10	0	6	0	16	0
CCAC Literacy Stand	ELLCO	NA	NA	29	27	29	27
	ARIC	NA	NA	29	27	29	27
	"Beliefs"	NA	NA	280	124	280	124
Faculty Institute	Faculty Institute	42	9	13	6	55	15
Focus Group	NA	NA	NA	4	NA	4	NA

Sample Sizes

It is important to note that pre-tests and post-tests were administered on all measures, and only data from those adults and children with complete data sets was included in the final analyses of the data. Due to attrition some individuals who completed pre-tests on some measures did not complete post-tests on these same measures. Therefore, the final sample sizes changed from the originally planned numbers and varied among measures.

Procedures

During the study period, CCSAR measured students' emerging literacy, their teachers' beliefs about effective ways to promote children's literacy, and professional development initiatives (i.e., LEEP, CCAC, Higher Education Faculty Institute). The research design was multifaceted. In the evaluation 219 preschool centers were involved during the course of the study. To measure changes in student outcomes, 44 *Peabody Picture Vocabulary Tests* (*PPVTs*) and 43 *Profiles of Early Literacy Development* (*PELDs*) were administered to preschool children whose teachers participated in LEEP. Twenty-four *PPVTs* and 23 *PELDs* were administered to preschool children in a Comparison group from centers that did not send their teachers to LEEP training or the literacy strand offered by CCAC. CCSAR staff visited classrooms and administered the *PPVT* and the *PELD* according to the administration procedures provided in the manuals. To measure the extent to which preschool teachers implement practices that promote children's emerging literacy CCSAR conducted 32 observations of LEEP classrooms, 27 observations of CCAC classrooms, and 35 observations of Comparison group classrooms. During the observations, the *Early Language and Literacy Classroom Observation* (*ELLCO*) was completed. To measure preschool teachers' and supervisors' beliefs about effective ways to promote children's literacy, CCSAR administered the *Literacy, Language and Curriculum Belief and Practices of Preschool Teachers* ("*Beliefs*") to 99 LEEP participants, 124 CCAC participants, and 34 Comparison group participants. In all, five focus group interviews were conducted. Two groups comprising both pre-school teachers and their supervisors who together participated in the LEEP training were interviewed. Members were selected randomly from various representative communities participating in Project STARS. Two groups of members/administrators representing the Connecticut State Department of Education participating in Project STARS were interviewed. Finally, one large group representing EDC, involved in either the delivery or the development of the early childhood literacy training, was interviewed.

It is important to note that pre-tests and post-tests were administered on all measures and only data for those adults and children for whom there were complete pre-test/post-test data sets were included in the final analysis. Due to attrition, some individuals who completed pre-tests on some measures did not complete post-tests on these same measures. Therefore, the final sample sizes changed from the original numbers and varied among measures.

The initial data analysis plan called for Hierarchical Linear Modeling (HLM) statistical procedures to be performed on the data. However, following consultation with an expert authority on HLM, it was determined that the available sample size would not allow for HLM statistical procedures to be conducted successfully. Pre-test/post-test changes within the intervention groups (LEEP and CCAC) and comparison groups were examined. Analysis of Covariance (ANCOVA) statistical procedures were conducted to address the research questions, which are stated in the Results section. ANCOVA procedures allowed for the statistical control of pre-test mean differences for the intervention and comparison groups on the outcome measures, as well as for examination of significant differences between the intervention and comparison groups on post-test mean scores for the outcome measures.

THE LEEP, CCAC, AND COMPARISON GROUPS

Project STARS provided professional development to preschool teachers. Consistent with this teacher-level intervention, CCSAR recruited preschool teachers who were comparable to the LEEP and CCAC preschool teachers. The preschool teachers from the LEEP, CCAC, and Comparison groups were from Connecticut's "priority" school districts. Priority school districts have high rates of "children in poverty or performing below remedial standards on state mastery examinations or high percentage concentrations of such children in communities" (Conn. Gen. Stat. §§ 10-266p through 10-266r).

To the *Literacy Language and Curriculum Belief and Practices of Preschool Teachers* survey, CCSAR had added a cover sheet that asked the

Table 6.2. Teachers' Educational Levels in Percentages

	High School or GED	CDA	Associates Degree	Bachelors Degree	Other
CCAC	49.5	12.5	13.1	15.5	9.4
LEEP*	17.2	17.9	21.4	24.8	18.6
Comparison	40.0	13.7	11.6	22.1	10.5

CCAC = 297, LEEP = 145, COMP = 95

participants to respond to demographic questions. The responses tended to be more similar than different. The following are the significant differences:

- The LEEP preschool teachers tended to have a significantly greater number of years in early education than the CCAC and Comparison teachers ($p < .001$).
- The LEEP and CCAC preschool teachers tended to have a significantly greater number of years in their current positions than the Comparison teachers ($p < .001$).
- LEEP preschool teachers tended to be bilingual at a significantly higher rate than the CCAC teachers ($p < .001$). The LEEP and Comparison teachers tended to be bilingual at the same rate. LEEP classrooms tended to have significantly more bilingual students than the CCAC and Comparison classrooms ($p < .011$ and $p < .045$).

The LEEP group contained both supervisors and teachers. Eighteen individuals in the LEEP group indicated that they had a Masters Degree. Five in the CCAC group indicated that they had a Masters Degree as well as ten in the Comparison group.

The Children

At the beginning of the study, the students whose teachers participated in LEEP tended to be at the 54th percentile on the *PPVT*. The Comparison group of students tended to be at the 56th percentile.

RESULTS

Children Outcomes

Evaluation Question # 1

Do children from classrooms of LEEP-trained teachers demonstrate significantly greater improvement on readiness for kindergarten language and literacy instruction, as measured by the Profile of Early Literacy Development (PELD) than a comparison group of children?

Profile of Early Literacy Development (PELD)

Only when there were two sets of *PELD* data available for a child (i.e., pre-test and post-test), were those data included in the final analysis. Significant pre-existing differences, in favor of the Comparison group existed on the pre-test administration of the *PELD*. However, as seen in Table 6.1, on the post-test of the *PELD*, (after the intervention program), the LEEP group had significantly narrowed the gap and had gained significantly more than their Comparison counterparts. LEEP participants also had a higher average rate of change than their peers in Comparison classrooms. The average rate of change was computed by averaging the differences of the *PELD* subscale scores observed over time (between the pre-test and post-test).

Prior to the LEEP intervention program, the Comparison group scored significantly higher on the following five aspects of the *PELD*: Phoneme Deletion ($p=.004$), Sense of Printed Language ($p<.001$), Print Concepts—Part I ($p<.001$), Print Concepts—Part II ($p=.022$), and Name Writing ($p=.001$). After the intervention program, the Comparison group scored significantly higher on only two dimensions of the *PELD*. These are Listening Comprehension ($p=.023$), and Sentence Dictation ($p=.012$).

Since letter identification is an important predictor of literacy, it is worthwhile to note that the LEEP group improved from 12.18 to 17.44. Pre-test and Post-test Mean Scores for LEEP and Comparison Children on the PELD are shown in figures 6.1 through 6.12. Note that the average rate of change was computed by averaging the differences of the *PELD* subscale scores observed over time (between the pre-test and post-test. The figures show that LEEP participants had a higher average rate of change than their peers in Comparison classrooms. The overall N for LEEP was 43 and the overall N for the Comparison group was 23. This is especially important with respect to the last several charts. For example, Sentence Dictation is the last subscale. Only 11 LEEP children and 16 Comparison children reached this subscale.

Pre-test differences on all outcome measures were controlled for through the Analysis of Covariance (ANCOVA) procedure. ANCOVA takes into account the pre-existing differences between intervention (i.e., LEEP) and comparison groups and then compares the groups' performances on the post-test measures.

Evaluation Question # 2

Do children from classrooms of LEEP-trained teachers demonstrate significantly greater improvement on readiness for kindergarten language and literacy instruction, as measured by the Peabody Picture Vocabulary Test (PPVT), than a Comparison group of children?

Peabody Picture Vocabulary Test (PPVT)

Only data for children who completed both the pre-test and the post-test on the *PPVT* were included in the final analysis. A non-significant, pre-existing difference, in favor of the Comparison group, existed on the pre-test administration of

Table 6.3. Pre-test and Post-test Mean Scores for LEEP and Comparison Children on the PELD

	PRE				Level of Significance of the Difference Between LEEP and Comparison on Pre-Test	POST				Level of Significance of the Difference Between LEEP and Comparison on Post-Test
	LEEP		Comparison			LEEP		Comparison		
	Mean	SD	Mean	SD		Mean	SD	Mean	SD	
Phoneme Deletion	9.69	4.60	12.07	3.04	0.004**	11.95	3.58	12.26	3.41	0.883
Rhyme Recognition	3.20	2.91	3.76	2.95	0.375	4.06	2.78	4.91	3.03	0.380
Rhyme Production	1.89	2.19	2.05	2.19	0.736	2.42	2.33	2.87	2.18	0.566
Reading Environmental Print	6.67	2.54	7.32	2.21	0.202	7.40	1.68	8.09	2.35	0.309
Sense of Printed Language	1.85	1.18	2.78	0.91	0.000**	1.89	1.14	2.22	1.20	0.800
Print Concepts (Part I)	1.11	1.45	2.51	1.29	0.000**	1.28	1.34	1.78	1.38	0.897
Print Concepts (Part II)	0.89	1.11	1.54	1.32	0.022*	0.96	1.09	1.57	1.41	0.304
Listening Comprehension	2.90	2.29	3.56	1.95	0.166	3.11	2.35	4.78	1.68	0.023*
Letter Identification	12.18	9.58	16.78	12.17	0.053	17.44	8.02	19.39	11.94	0.392
Name Writing	3.40	2.56	5.00	1.69	0.001**	4.55	2.28	5.14	1.67	0.563
Sentence Dictation	0.89	1.42	1.50	3.59	0.403	0.18	0.40	2.00	3.50	0.012*

*Difference is significant at the 0.05 level
**Difference is significant at the 0.01 level

120   Chapter Six

the *PPVT*. As seen in Table 6.4, on the post-test of the *PPVT*, the LEEP group had not significantly narrowed the gap and did not gain significantly more than their Comparison counterparts.

Age was ruled out as an explanatory factor in the Comparison group's performance on their post *PPVT* scores vs. the LEEP group's scores. Analysis of Co-variances (ANOVA) was conducted on the student's *PPVT* Raw scores by their current age at the time of evaluation. This analysis

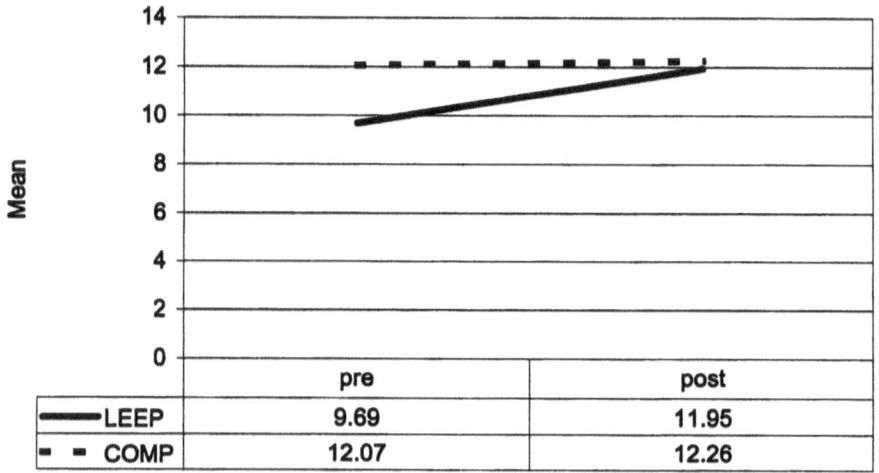
Figure 6.1.   PELD-Phoneme Deletion.

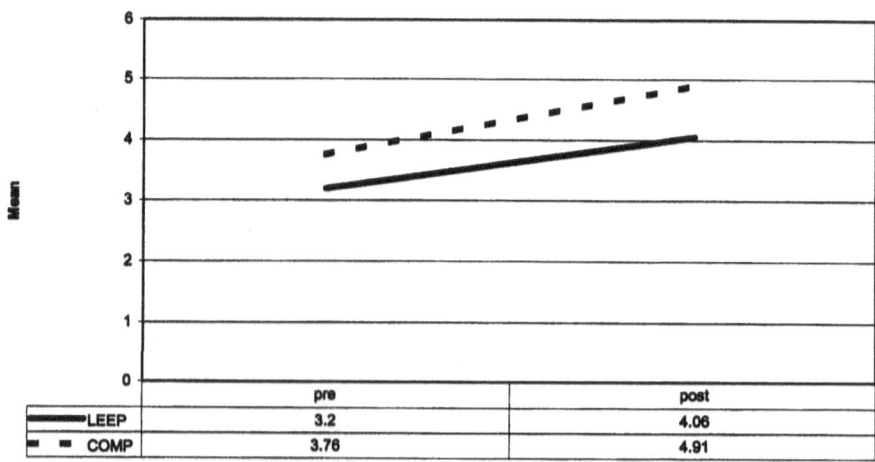
Figure 6.2.   PELD-Rhyme Recognition.

Evaluation Study of Striving to Achieve Reading Success Project STARS 121

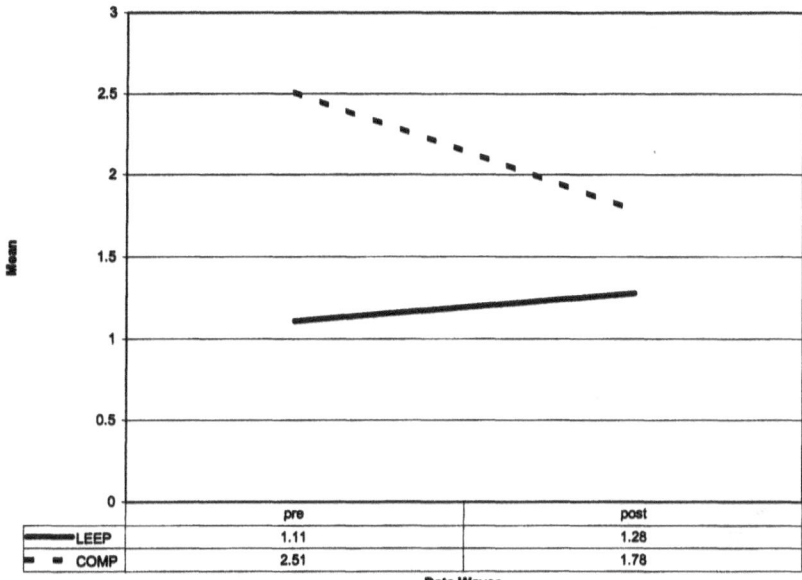

Figure 6.3. PELD-Print Concepts (Part I).

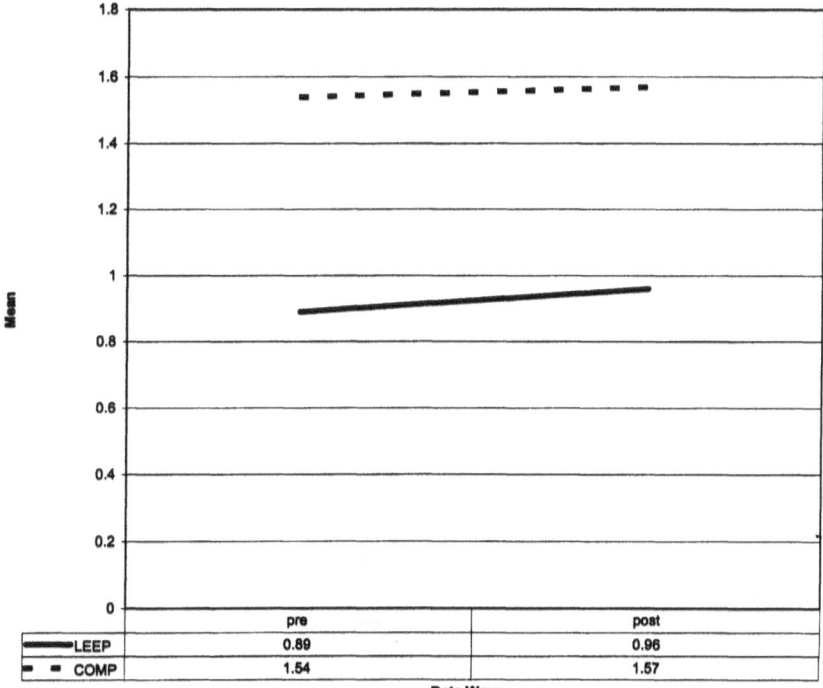

Figure 6.4. PELD-Print Concepts (Part II).

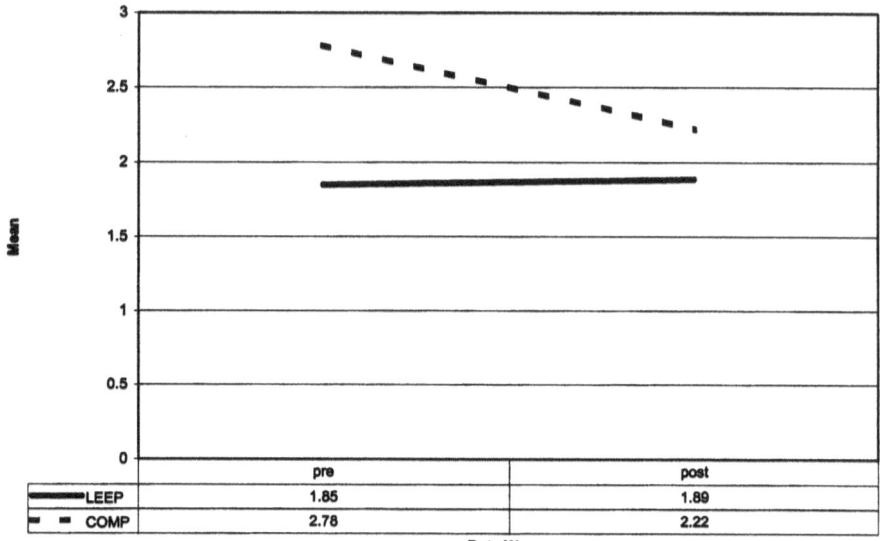

Figure 6.5. PELD-Sense of Printed Language.

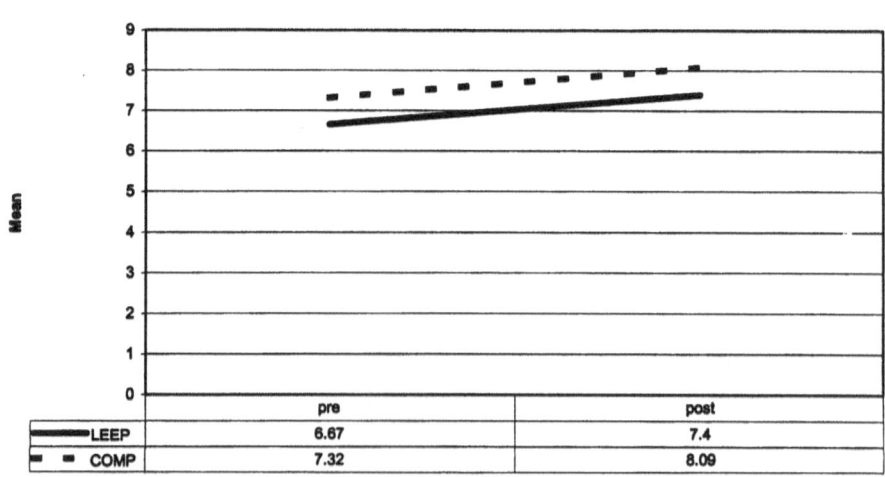

Figure 6.6. PELD-Reading Environmental Print.

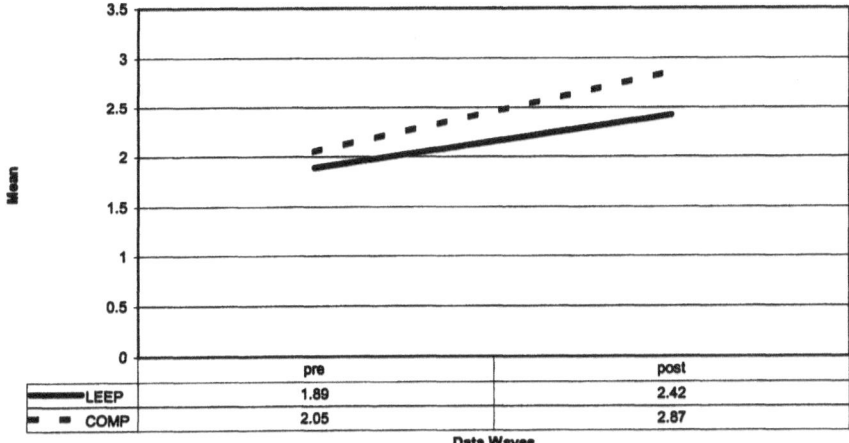

Figure 6.7. PELD-Rhyme Production.

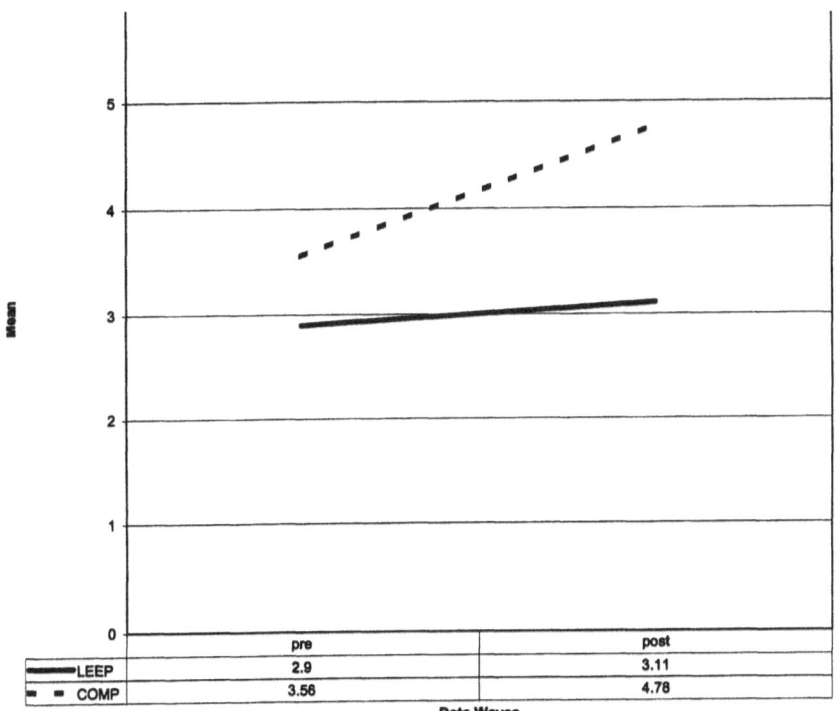

Figure 6.8. PELD-Listening Comprehension.

124   *Chapter Six*

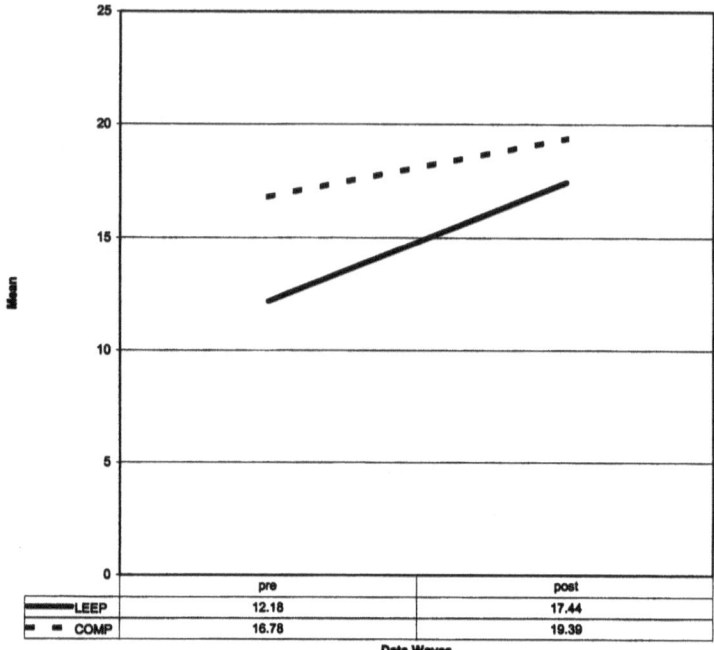

Figure 6.9. PELD-Letter Identification.

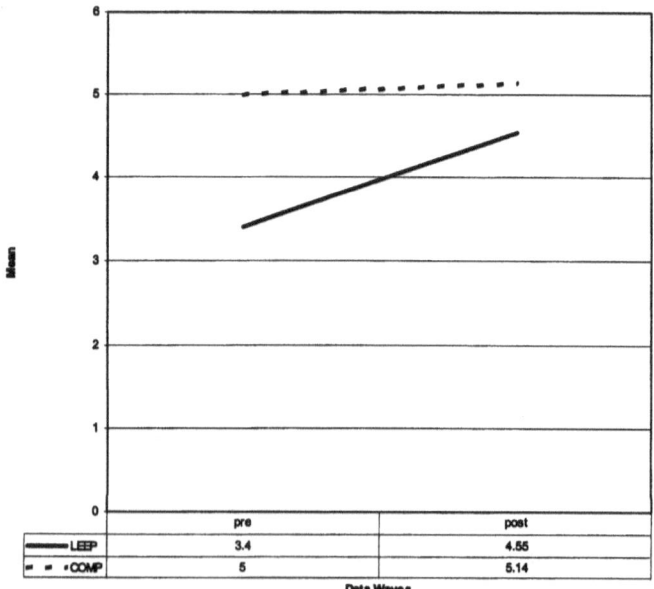

Figure 6.10. PELD-Name Writing.

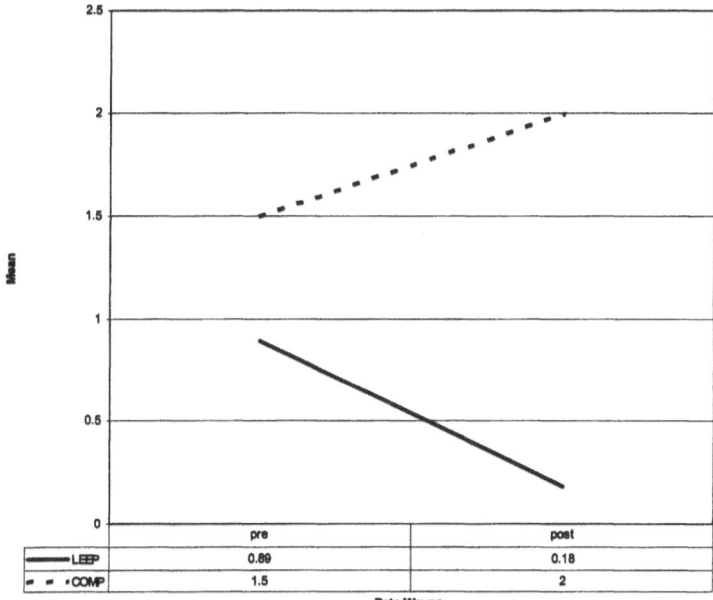

Figure 6.11. PELD-Sentence Dictation.

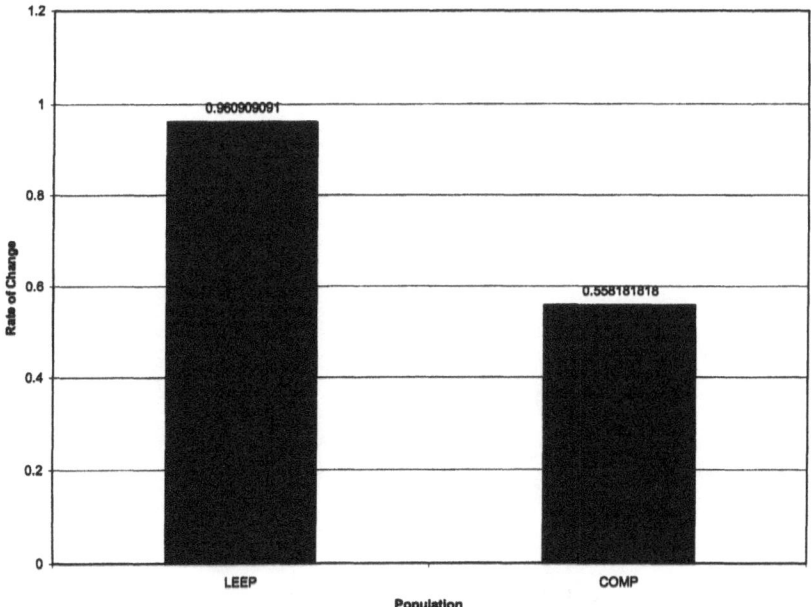

Figure 6.12. PELD-Average Rate of Change: LEEP vs. COMP.

Table 6.4. Pre-test and Post-test Mean Scores for LEEP and Comparison Children on the PPVT

	PRE				Level of Significance of the Difference Between LEEP and Comparison on Pre-Test	POST				Level of Significance of the Difference Between LEEP and Comparison on Post-Test
	LEEP		Comparison			LEEP		Comparison		
	Mean	SD	Mean	SD		Mean	SD	Mean	SD	
PPVT – Raw Score	58.61	(22.81)	60.17	(18.54)	.720	58.84	(24.08)	65.00	(16.56)	0.058
PPVT - Percentile	54.07	(32.27)	55.59	(25.99)	.805	50.87	(31.97)	62.50	(22.53)	0.049*

LEEP: N=44 Comparison: N=24
*Difference is significant at the 0.05 level
[Note: the time frame between the pre-test and the post-test was similar for the LEEP and Comparison groups]

Evaluation Study of Striving to Achieve Reading Success Project STARS 127

revealed that for the overall population (both LEEP and Comparison) as students' age increased so did their post PPVT scores ($p<.001$). A subsequent analysis was then performed to determine if there was a significant difference in age between LEEP and Comparison children. Independent Samples T-Tests showed that there was no significant difference in age between LEEP and Comparison children.

When looking at the *PPVT* scores of the LEEP and Comparison groups, it is worthwhile to underscore that the standard deviations of both groups show that the range of scores was from the lowest percentiles to the highest percentiles. One LEEP student, for example, scored higher than all of the Comparison group groups?.

For this reason, it was worthwhile to take a look at the LEEP *PPVT* scores by city. Site A was a LEEP site during the first year. Later, LEEP training was moved to another city. Before the move, pre- and post-tests were administered to three students. These scores showed a decrease from a mean of 48 at the point of the pre-test to 39 at the point of the post-test. Site B scored very highly on the pre-test (85). In fact, both the pre-test scores and post-test scores of the ten Site B students were higher than any other LEEP site. However, there was a decrease in scores from 85 to 79 over the course of the study. Site C's twenty-five students experienced a slight increase in scores from the pre-test (51.40) to the time of the post-test (51.48). Site D's six students experienced positive change from the pre-test (59) to the post-test (64).

Figures 6.13 and 6.14 depict the two sites in which positive change on the students' *PPVT* scores were observed.

It is also important to keep in mind the contextual factors that may have influenced the results. For example, LEEP classrooms tended to have

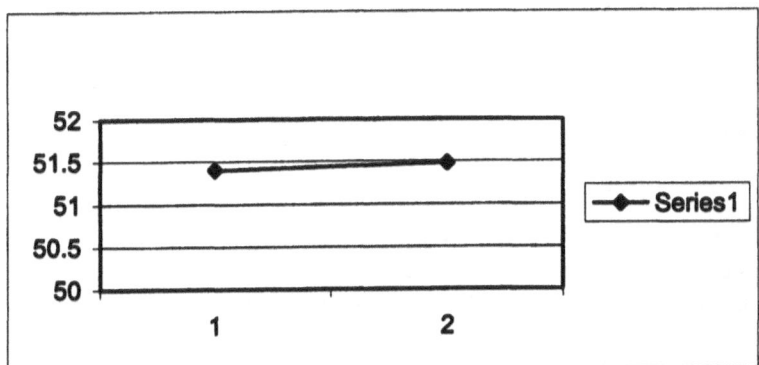

Figure 6.13. Site C.

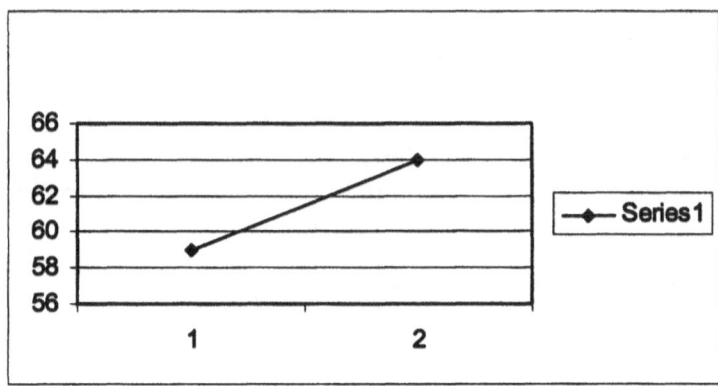

Figure 6.14. Site D.

significantly more bilingual students than the CCAC and Comparison classrooms ($p < .011$ and $p < .045$). For example, 22.7% of the LEEP preschool teachers indicated that *most* of the children under their care were bilingual. By way of contrast, only 9% of CCAC preschool teachers and 6.8% of the Comparison teachers indicated that *most* were bilingual.

Due to the low socioeconomic status (SES) of the six priority school districts included in this study, the state targeted these districts for special attention and services. Thus, SES is not a confounding variable in this study because all the school districts tend to have SES levels that are more similar than different. However, , the "Comparison" parents who consented to allow their children to be evaluated—without an incentive to do so—could have differed in some important way from the parents who did not agree. Another interpretation of the data is that the *PPVT* lacks the sensitivity to truly capture children's underlying language development and literacy learning.

Classroom Environment Outcome

Evaluation Question # 3

Do classrooms staffed by participants in the LEEP training show greater improvement in promoting literacy learning environments, as measured by the Early Language and Literacy Classroom Observation (ELLCO), in comparison to classrooms not staffed by teachers trained in LEEP or CCAC (i.e., the Comparison group)?

Early Language and Literacy Classroom Observation

ELLCO Subscales. The three subscales of the *ELLCO* are (1) General Classroom Environment Total, (2) Language, Literacy, and Curriculum Total, and (3) Classroom Observation Total. Analyses were conducted to discern if there were significant differences between the LEEP and Comparison groups on their scores on these three *ELLCO* subscales.

Table 6.5 shows that LEEP classrooms had significantly higher post-test scores than the Comparison Group on all three subscales of the ELLCO ("Between Group Analyses")

Analyses of Co-Variances (ANCOVA) were conducted to determine whether significant differences exist between the LEEP and Comparison groups on the post-test. The ANCOVA method takes into account only those cases where both pre- and post-test scores exist. For the purpose of the analysis, the LEEP group consisted of 32 pairs of pre- and post-test scores and the Comparison group consisted of 35 pairs of pre- and post-test scores.

Whereas the LEEP and the Comparison groups started at the same level, at the time of the post-test, there were significant differences between the two groups. On all three subscales, the LEEP group had significantly higher mean scores. The *ELLCO* was developed by the same organization that designed the LEEP training (EDC). As such, it is purportedly a suitable and sensitive measure of the impact of the LEEP training in the classroom. The findings of the *ELLCO* suggest that the LEEP training influenced the supervisors' and teachers' practices in the classroom.

A "within group" analysis was conducted with only the LEEP group to see the extent to which this group changed over time—without comparing the group to another one (e.g., the Comparison Group or CCAC). Table 6.6 shows the results of the LEEP within group analysis.

Evaluation Question # 4

Do classrooms staffed by participants in the CCAC training show greater improvement in promoting literacy learning environments, as measured by the Early Language and Literacy Classroom Observation (ELLCO), in comparison to classrooms not staffed by teachers trained in CCAC or LEEP (i.e., the Comparison group)?

Table 6.7 shows that pre-existing differences in favor of the Comparison classrooms existed on two *ELLCO* subscales (Language, Literacy, and Curriculum Total and Classroom Observation Total). At the time of the post-test,

Table 6.5. Pre-test and Post-test Mean Scores for LEEP and Comparison Classrooms on the ELLCO

	PRE				Level of Significance of the Difference Between LEEP and Comparison on Pre-Test	POST				Level of Significance of the Difference Between LEEP and Comparison on Post-Test
	LEEP		Comparison			LEEP		Comparison		
	Mean	SD	Mean	SD		Mean	SD	Mean	SD	
General Classroom Environment Total	18.79	3.60	18.27	3.72	0.547	19.84	3.47	17.91	3.74	0.039*
Language, Literacy, and Curriculum Total	24.48	8.01	25.76	5.48	0.421	28.28	5.71	25.57	7.07	0.046*
Classroom Observation Total	45.88	11.60	46.54	9.14	0.786	50.72	9.05	45.91	11.05	0.032*

*Difference is significant at the 0.05 level

Table 6.6. Pre-test and Post-test Mean Scores for LEEP Classrooms on the ELLCO Subscales

	Pre	SD	Post	SD	Significance
General Classroom Environment Total	19.00	3.45	19.84	3.47	0.087
Language, Literacy, and Curriculum Total	24.84	7.86	28.28	5.71	0.017*
Classroom Observation Total	46.50	11.22	50.72	9.05	0.017*

N=32 *Difference is significant at the 0.05 level

the CCAC group had closed the gap. No significant differences between the groups were found on any of the subscales.

Tables 6.8 and 6.9 show the results of the within group analysis for the CCAC and Comparison groups. CCAC improved on Language, Literacy, and Curriculum Total. The Comparison group did not improve.

Teacher and Supervisors Outcome

Evaluation Question # 5

Do participants who receive LEEP training show significantly increased knowledge and understanding of research-based approaches to developing children's language and literacy, school readiness, and childhood pedagogy, as measured by the *Literacy Language and Curriculum Belief and Practices of Preschool Teachers* ("Beliefs"), than a comparison group of teachers? The "Beliefs" is a self-report instrument.

Literacy Language and Curriculum Belief and Practices of Preschool Teachers ("Beliefs")

Table 6.10 shows that the LEEP group significantly improved on one of three "Beliefs" variables (Within Group Analysis)

Evaluation Question # 6

Do participants who receive CCAC training show significantly increased knowledge and understanding of research-based approaches to developing children's language and literacy, school readiness, and childhood pedagogy, as measured by the *Literacy Language and Curriculum Belief and Practices of Preschool Teachers* ("Beliefs"), than a comparison group of teachers?

Table 6.11 shows that the CCAC group significantly improved on two of the three *Beliefs* variables.

Table 6.7. Pre-test and Post-test Mean Scores for CCAC and Comparison Classrooms on the ELLCO

	PRE				Level of Significance of the Difference Between LEEP and Comparison on Pre-Test	POST				Level of Significance of the Difference Between LEEP and Comparison on Post-Test
	LEEP		Comparison			LEEP		Comparison		
	Mean	SD	Mean	SD		Mean	SD	Mean	SD	
General Classroom Environment Total	16.86	3.64	18.27	3.72	0.121	15.89	3.25	17.91	3.74	0.082
Language, Literacy, and Curriculum Total	22.38	4.37	25.76	5.48	0.006**	24.41	4.95	25.57	7.07	0.834
Classroom Observation Total	41.48	8.24	46.54	9.14	0.019*	42.78	8.23	45.91	11.05	0.629

*Difference is significant at the 0.05 leve
**Difference is significant at the 0.01 level

Table 6.8. Pre-test and Post-test Mean Scores for CCAC Classrooms on the ELLCO Subscales

	Pre	SD	Post	SD	Significance
General Classroom Environment Total	16.81	3.71	15.89	3.25	0.215
Language, Literacy, and Curriculum Total	22.22	4.49	24.41	4.95	0.040*
Classroom Observation Total	41.33	8.50	42.78	8.23	0.443

N=35 *Difference is significant at the 0.05 level

Table 6.9. Pre-test and Post-test Mean Scores for Comparison Classrooms on the ELLCO Subscales

	Pre	SD	Post	SD	Significance
General Classroom Environment Total	18.46	3.91	17.91	3.74	0.509
Language, Literacy, and Curriculum Total	25.94	5.66	25.57	7.07	0.772
Classroom Observation Total	46.91	9.54	45.91	11.05	0.632

N=27

Table 6.10. Pre-test and Post-test Mean Scores for LEEP on the "Beliefs" Variables

	Pre	SD	Post	SD	Significance
Literacy Development	3.69	0.26	3.79	0.29	0.014*
Curriculum Planning and Implementation	3.79	0.29	3.80	0.51	0.770
Professional Support	3.96	0.64	4.04	0.67	0.268

N=99 *Difference is significant at the 0.05 level

Table 6.11. Pre-test and Post-test Mean Scores for CCAC on the "Beliefs" Variables

	Pre	SD	Post	SD	Significance
Literacy Development	3.46	0.32	3.62	0.31	0.000*
Curriculum Planning and Implementation	3.65	0.41	3.78	0.42	0.005**
Professional Support	4.05	0.63	4.10	0.68	0.469

N=124 **Difference is significant at the 0.01 level

134   Chapter Six

Table 6.12. Pre-test and Post-test Mean Scores for the Comparison Group on the "Beliefs" Variables

	Pre	SD	Post	SD	Significance
Literacy Development	3.61	0.30	3.67	0.27	0.179
Curriculum Planning and Implementation	3.80	0.34	3.88	0.22	0.258
Professional Support	4.26	0.43	4.05	0.41	0.232

N=34

Table 6.12 shows that the Comparison group did not show significant improvement on any of the three *Beliefs* variables.

The Higher Education Faculty Institute

Evaluation Question # 7

Did faculty who participated in the Higher Education Faculty Institute incorporate into their instruction more research-based content knowledge on early literacy and language development?

The following information is based on the responses of 55 individuals in total. During Year One; 42 individuals completed the *Higher Education Faculty Institute Assessment* that was administered during the first wave of data collection (the "pre-test"). Of these individuals, nine completed the assessment during the second wave of data collection. During Year Two, 13 completed the assessment during the first wave of data collection and six completed the assessment during the second wave.

Background Information

- Postsecondary Institution (n=54): 24.1% were employed at 4–year private institutes of higher education, 27.8% from 4–year public, 1.9% from 2–year private, 38.9% from 2–year public, and 7.4% indicated "Other"
- Title (n=52): 16.4% were Professors, 12.7% Associate Professor, 25.5% Assistant Professors, 16.4% Instructors, and 23.6% responded "Other"
- Employed (n=54): 78.2% are employed full-time and 20.0% part-time
- Years in current position (n=55): Mean response to years in current position was 4.4 years, the minimum was 1 year, and the maximum was 27 years
- Years in early childhood education (n=55): Mean response was 7.2 years; minimum was 1 year, and maximum 33 years

- Gender (n=55): 7.3% were male, 92.7% were female
- Highest Degree Earned (n=53): 24.5% of the respondents earned a Ph.D., 15.1% an Ed.D., 22.6% a M.A., 22.6%, a M.S., 7.5% a B.A., and 7.5% responded "Other"
- Bilingual (n=55): 90.9% said "No" and 9.1% said "Yes."

Participants at the Higher Education Faculty Institute tended to include the following content in their courses:

- Conversations with children—what does and does not facilitate language growth at different developmental stages
- Characteristics and implementation of effective book reading
- What parents can do at home to help children's language and literacy development
- The nature and development of "emerging writing"

Participants tended not to include the following content in their courses:

- How best to foster the language and literacy development in children learning English as a new language (English Language Learners = ELL)
- The developmental periods that ELL children experience as they learn English

Given the relatively limited sample size, rigorous statistical procedures could not be conducted. Still, it is possible to make a few observations. Participants were asked to indicate the extent to which they use in course syllabus/instruction.

- "The nature and development of emergent writing." Whereas during the first wave of data collection 16% indicated that they never or rarely did so, 0% indicated "Never" or "Rarely" during the second wave.
- "Stimulating the visual knowledge of print in children (getting marks to look like print, etc.)." Whereas during the first wave of data collection 35% indicated that they often did so, 54% indicated "Often" during the second wave.
- "Instruction in Phonological Awareness." Whereas during the first wave of data collection 6% indicated that they never do, 0% indicated "Never" during the second wave. The same change was noted also for "How sound affects writing."

Table 6.13. Responses During the First Wave of the Faculty Institute Assessment

Degree to which you currently include this content/skill in your syllabus/instruction (in %'s):

	Never	Rarely	Sometimes	Often	Mean	SD
The nature and development of "emerging writing"	2.0	14.0	32.0	52.0	3.34	0.80
Stimulating the visual knowledge of print in children (getting marks to look like print, etc.)	11.8	19.6	33.3	35.3	2.92	1.02
What print conventions are (return sweep, top to bottom, etc.)	11.8	27.5	29.4	31.4	2.80	1.02
Fostering and assessing letter knowledge in children (letter names, visual image of shapes, etc.)	4.0	10.0	50.0	36.0	3.18	0.77
Developmental stages of phonological awareness	5.9	15.7	39.2	39.2	3.12	0.89
Instruction in phonological awareness	6.0	14.0	38.0	42.0	3.16	0.89
How sound affects writing	6.0	22.0	36.0	36.0	3.02	0.91
Word creation strategies (visual design, syllabic coding, letter string, etc.)	7.8	33.3	25.5	33.3	2.84	0.99
Conversations with (input to) children - what does and does not facilitate language growth at different developmental stages	0	7.8	29.4	62.7	3.55	0.64
Research on how to facilitate use of more advanced oral language skills	4.2	14.6	50.0	31.3	3.08	0.79
The different forms of "personal narratives" and their use	12.0	30.0	44.0	14.0	2.60	0.88
Components of "curriculum-related" conversations	10.0	30.0	42.0	18.0	2.68	0.89

Topic	%	%	%	%	Mean	SD
Research-proven strategies to systematically enhance vocabulary knowledge	4.0	36.0	28.0	32.0	2.88	0.92
Research on selecting books for 3 to 5 year olds, including access to current resources	6.0	14.0	32.0	48.0	3.22	0.91
Different book genres and their specific uses and benefits	3.9	15.7	25.5	54.9	3.31	0.88
Characteristics and implementation of effective book reading	3.9	5.9	33.3	56.9	3.43	0.78
Developmental constraints in influencing how best to allocate time to instructional activities (minutes children can listen to a story in a group or alone, minutes spent in dramatic play, etc.)	3.9	15.7	37.3	43.1	3.20	0.85
Research-based criteria for developing, implementing, and assessing preschool curricula that optimize early language and literacy	10.0	26.0	40.0	24.0	2.78	0.93
The research-based criteria for selecting curriculum topics	5.9	37.3	39.2	17.6	2.69	0.84
Approaches to create a home-school environment that promotes language and literacy development	6.0	10.0	40.0	44.0	3.22	0.86
How best to foster the language and literacy development in children learning English as a new language (English Language Learners - ELL)	11.8	47.1	27.5	13.7	2.43	0.88
What parents can do at home to help children's language and literacy development	5.9	3.9	37.3	52.9	3.37	0.82
The developmental periods that ELL children experience as they learn English	16.3	36.7	32.7	14.3	2.45	0.94

Table 6.14. Responses During the Second Wave of the Faculty Institute Assessment

Degree to which you currently include this content/skill in your syllabus/instruction (in %'s):

	Never	Rarely	Sometimes	Often	Mean	SD
The nature and development of "emerging writing"	0	0	38.5	61.5	3.61	.5
Stimulating the visual knowledge of print in children (getting marks to look like print, etc.)	7.7	15.4	23.1	53.8	3.23	1.01
What print conventions are (return sweep, top to bottom, etc.)	7.7	23.1	38.5	30.8	3.00	1.00
Fostering and assessing letter knowledge in children (letter names, visual image of shapes, etc.)	7.7	23.1	30.8	38.5	3.00	1.00
Developmental stages of phonological awareness	7.7	15.4	46.2	30.8	3.00	.91
Instruction in phonological awareness	0	7.7	61.5	30.8	3.23	.59
How sound affects writing	0	7.7	61.5	30.8	3.23	.59
Word creation strategies (visual design, syllabic coding, letter string, etc.)	0	30.8	46.2	23.1	2.92	.75
Conversations with (input to) children - what does and does not facilitate language growth at different developmental stages	0	7.7	23.1	69.2	3.61	.65
Research on how to facilitate use of more advanced oral language skills	0	15.4	38.5	46.2	3.30	.75
The different forms of "personal narratives" and their use	7.7	15.4	61.5	15.4	2.85	.80
Components of "curriculum-related" conversations	7.7	7.7	46.2	38.5	3.15	.90
Research-proven strategies to systematically enhance vocabulary knowledge	7.7	15.4	38.5	38.5	3.08	.95

Topic					
Research on selecting books for 3 to 5 year olds, including access to current resources	0	15.4	23.1	61.5	3.46	.78
Different book genres and their specific uses and benefits	0	0	38.5	61.5	3.61	.50
Characteristics and implementation of effective book reading	0	8.3	25.0	66.7	3.58	.67
Developmental constraints in influencing how best to allocate time to instructional activities (minutes children can listen to a story in a group or alone, minutes spent in dramatic play, etc.)	0	23.1	30.8	46.2	3.23	.83
Research-based criteria for developing, implementing, and assessing preschool curricula that optimize early language and literacy	15.4	0	30.8	53.8	3.23	1.09
The research-based criteria for selecting curriculum topics	7.7	15.4	30.8	46.2	3.15	.98
Approaches to create a home-school environment that promotes language and literacy development	0	7.7	38.5	53.8	3.46	.66
How best to foster the language and literacy development in children learning English as a new language (English Language Learners - ELL)	7.7	23.1	38.5	30.8	2.92	.95
What parents can do at home to help children's language and literacy development	0	0	38.5	61.5	3.61	.50
The developmental periods that ELL children experience as they learn English	15.4	30.8	23.1	30.8	2.69	1.10

- "Research on how to facilitate use of more advanced oral language skills." Whereas during the first wave of data collection 31% indicated that they often did so, 46% indicated "Often" during the second wave.
- "Components of curriculum-related conversations." Whereas during the first wave of data collection 18% indicated that they often did so, 39% indicated "Often" during wave two.
- "Research on selecting books for 3 to 5 year olds, including access to current resources." Whereas during the first wave of data collection 48% indicated that they often did so, 62% indicated "Often" during wave two.
- "Research–based criteria for developing, implementing, and assessing preschool curricular that optimize early language and literacy." Whereas during the first wave of data collection 24% indicated that they often did so, 54% indicated "Often" during wave two.
- "The research-based criteria for selecting curriculum topics." Whereas during the first wave of data collection 18% indicated that they often did so, 46% indicated "Often" during wave two.
- "How best to foster the language and literacy development in children learning English as a new language." Whereas during the first wave of data collection, 14% indicated that they often did so, 31% indicated "Often" during wave two.
- "The developmental periods that ELL children experience as they learn English." Whereas during the first wave of data collection, 14% indicated that they often did so, 31% indicated "Often" during wave two.

These observations suggest that participants in the Higher Education Faculty Institute incorporated into their instruction more research-based content knowledge on early literacy and language development.

PROCESS EVALUATION

Focus Group Interviews

The process evaluation examined the nature and quality of program implementation. A series of focus group interviews was conducted to facilitate the evaluation team's understanding of the perspectives of Project STARS' partners and participants. Interview questions were designed to help understand the impact of the LEEP training on early childhood teachers, supervisors, classrooms, and preschool children exposed to the new techniques. For example, CCSAR's evaluation team sought to know what EDC, the designers of LEEP, had as their original goal in preparing the

LEEP course for the early childhood teachers and their supervisors. In other words, what did EDC expect after the course was completed and preschool teachers and supervisors worked in early childhood classrooms? What impact did they foresee this specific training to have on preschool children's language and literacy development? The interview protocol for all groups included such questions as:

- In your view, did the course meet the intended objectives for enhancing preschool vocabulary and literacy?
- How was the course received by the preschool teachers and by the supervisors?
- What was new/improved about this language and literacy course?
- What changes in early literacy development may be anticipated in the classrooms as a consequence of preschool teachers and supervisors experiencing the course?

Implementation Assessment

Five focus groups were conducted. Two groups comprising both preschool teachers and their supervisors who together participated in the LEEP training were interviewed. Members were selected randomly from various representative communities participating in Project STARS. Two groups of members/administrators representing the Connecticut State Department of Education participating in Project STARS were interviewed. Finally, one large group of membership representing EDC involved in either the delivery or the development of the early childhood literacy training was interviewed. Through the focus group interviews, the evaluation team addressed whether there was a consistency among the three broad groups regarding:

- shared expectations for the LEEP training
- perceptions of the success of the training itself
- how this design of literacy training may have differed from other professional development literacy experiences preschool teachers and supervisors had attended in the past
- how classrooms may be expected to be impacted in terms of enhanced language and literacy as a consequence of the training, and
- what effect may be anticipated for the preschool children as a consequence of teachers and supervisors participation in the LEEP training?

Questions were not distributed prior to the interview itself and consequently responses were spontaneous and rich with candor.

The diverse perspectives of the groups provided rich content. Equally as exciting as the EDC group, was the enthusiasm of each of the groups of early childhood teachers and supervisors, most of whom had never before met. Even though they worked in different cities and were in different phases of the training, they shared a common experience with similar rewards and challenges. For them, this was a first time opportunity to share with colleagues from across the State what they had learned, how they implemented those teachings, and what they saw as results.

Teachers appeared eager to share their experience in the LEEP course. In a large group format they validated the similarities and differences of their experiences with those of other preschool teachers who experienced similar training. They addressed and discussed their challenges in detail, but the overall expression from the teachers and supervisors was overwhelmingly positive. Indeed, one teacher commented, "I revel every day that I go into the classroom. I wish every teacher had this opportunity!"

The Connecticut State Department of Education, EDC, and the early childhood educators and their supervisors shared the same goal: to increase children's learning in the areas of language and literacy development during their preschool year, thereby enhancing their kindergarten and primary school experience. LEEP was successful, according to all the groups. The groups also had concerns and suggestions for improvements. These concerns and suggestions will be detailed below.

EDC and the Connecticut State Department of Education were aware of some of the challenges that the teachers and supervisors experienced. For example, challenges were encountered with the videotaping, and expectations for evaluation around the videotaping (this was new for almost all the participants). Teachers were concerned about whether their performance in the training and in the videotaping had professional and job-related implications. Other issues included the level of difficulty and pace of the course content, the amount of work/homework required, the condensation of the course, and the receiving of feedback with superiors present.

EDC felt excited about what was accomplished through the LEEP training. One member shared, "It changes the [teacher's] relationship with children in the classroom. It makes them into reflective practitioners... For supervisors, it really changes the way that they work with teachers."

EDC articulated its challenges in teaching participants with a broad range of skills. This particularly impacted the written assignments. Whenever possible, accommodations were made for participants in need. EDC members were very sensitive to the diversity of skills found in the classroom. They struggled with appropriate methods of feedback to facilitate participants' learning and keep motivational energy high. One participant in the group told us, "It's very hard to evaluate people's work when you know they're probably doing the best they can, and you know they're learning an enormous amount from where they started." Descriptions of the ways instructors sought to accommodate students' needs in the LEEP course will be detailed in subsequent sections.

An important part of the LEEP training was the opportunity for supervisors to meet together, apart from the teachers, to discuss supervisory and administrative issues. Through these meetings, supervisors supported each other. Typically, such an opportunity to meet with other Early Childhood Directors/ supervisors is rare, and supervisors appreciated it.

Teachers and supervisors reported feeling validated for the changes they instituted in their teaching as a result of the LEEP course. They had a solid rationale for teaching language and literacy that could be shared with parents and others. If their classrooms were structured differently in their appearances, if their lessons looked and were approached differently from what is traditional, teachers and supervisors understood why and could explain the purpose to others. EDC as well as the teacher and supervisor groups shared that having that rationale securely understood, gave license to teachers to risk trying some different, new, and creative early language and literacy strategies.

The Connecticut Department of Education members felt that teachers were making early literacy strides in classroom teaching. They felt that teachers had begun important work and that children are likely to continue to make steady gains. Other members candidly expressed their concern about follow-up in the classrooms once the training had been completed. It was hoped that the practices once introduced, would continue.

Each group was interviewed for one session that lasted approximately ninety minutes. Care was taken to hear from all of the participants in each group. In every group participants were most eager to share their perceptions and views. Transcripted data and notations have been analyzed, distilled, and summarized in the following pages.

GENERAL TRENDS

Challenges

- Rigors of the college course and required writing and reading
- Program supervisors felt directed to this professional development opportunity and thereby less committed than those who volunteered to participate
- Commitment level impacted recruitment and enrollment encountered in some cities

- Lack of support from schools in some cities
- Weekends difficult for many to attend classes after a full-time work week
- Not enough time between the sessions and homework feedback to make corrections
- More informal talk time with instructors for technical assistance needed
  Sessions too condensed
- Timing difficult for teachers to finish all assignments with their normal end-of-the-year responsibilities
- Training more intrusive than what participants originally anticipated
- Clarity of grading rubric for first assignment. Anxiety inducing for many to turn in an assignment to be graded by an unknown teacher
- Separate teacher and supervision group sessions were suspect
- Perceptions of unequal or inconsistent assignments
- When three instructors/professors were co-teaching, the quality of instruction was perceived as unequal
- One higher education institution was perceived as unsupportive
- Maintaining teachers' level of trust that supervisory feedback is not professionally evaluative

Strengths

- Specific language and literacy training
- Research-based training
- Understanding child development in terms of language and literacy
- Learning to enhance language, print, and literacy in classrooms
- Training material presented clearly; easy to read, easy to follow
- Time allowed to practice new material in the classroom
- Length of class time
- Access to teachers
- College credit
- Opportunities for creative ways for the course participants to communicate or present their assignments (i.e., redo, telephone, conferences, videotaping, interview, photographs). This was especially important for the "nontraditional" higher education students.
- Rationale for early literacy experiences vital to school success
- Site visits offer specific feedback
- Preschool teachers felt validated for the literacy instruction that they are already implementing in their classrooms
- The supervisors' presence in the course provided the preschool teachers with the administrative support that they need to change
- Participants receive specific feedback

- Participants receive feedback through a variety of methods
- Participants provided with opportunities to receive help
- Supervisors participate in training
- Teachers have new opportunities to work closely with their supervisors
- Supervisors have new opportunities to improve their supervision
- Supervisors learn and practice conferencing with teachers
- Children practice oral and written language in new ways in the classroom
- Children are exposed to new and varied pre-literacy and literacy experiences
- Children show classroom enthusiasm

The strengths of the LEEP training suggest the capacity to bring about significant long-term language and literacy change in preschool classrooms. The strength in the training model itself, cited repeatedly by Connecticut Department of Education administrators, is to unite the training of the supervisors with that of their teachers. Supervisors are likely to have lasting impact on the early childhood facility in which they work. Staff/faculty may change and turnover. A LEEP-trained supervisor is likely to introduce critical concepts of language and literacy to any new early childhood staff. If the supervisor receives research-based training in implementing language and literacy into the preschool classroom, language and literacy concepts are woven into a concrete planned curriculum. Through the training, supervisors are provided with the knowledge of how and why to promote literacy in their early childhood centers.

When perusing a list of strengths in bulleted format, it is possible to miss the enthusiasm exhibited throughout the focus group discussions and the potential positive results for children, not only in preschool, but also in the grades to follow. Teachers, without exception, recommended the training and felt that their preschool children benefited directly.

REFERENCES

Cochran-Smith, M. (1991). Learning to teach against the grain. *Harvard Educational Review, 61*(3), 279–310.

Cochran-Smith, M. & Lytle, S. (1990). Research on teaching and teacher research: The issues that divide. *Educational Researcher, 19*(2), 2–11.

Connecticut State Department of Education. (2000). Hartford: *Connecticut's blueprint for reading achievement: The report of the early reading success panel*

Connecticut State Department of Education. Early literacy: Early literacy development: A focus on preschool. Retrieved on 6/12/2005 from, http://www.state.ct.us/sde

Dickinson, D. K. (2001). Putting the pieces together: The impact of preschool on children's language and literacy development in kindergarten. In D. K. Dickinson & P. O. Tabor (Eds.), *Preparing for literacy at home and school: The critical role of language development in the preschool years*. Baltimore: Brookes.

Dickinson, D. K., Miller, C. M. & Anastaspoulos, L. P. (2000, June). *The impact of the Literacy Enrichment Environment Program on teachers, supervisors, and children*. Poster session presented at the annual conferennce of the National Association for the Education of Young Children's National Institute for Early Childhood Professional Development, San Francisco.

Dickinson, D. & Sprague K. (2002). The nature and impact of early childhood care environments on the language and early literacy development of children from low-income families. In S. Neuman & D. Dickinson (Eds.), *Handbook of early literacy research* (pp. 263–280). New York: The Guilford Press.

Gallimore, R., & Goldenberg. R (1993). Activity settings of early literacy: Home and school factors in children's emergent literacy. In E. Forman, N. Minick, & C.A. Stone, *Contexts for learning* (pp. 315–335). New York: Oxford University Press.

Leont'ev., A. N. (1979). The problem of activity in psychology. In J.V. Wertsch (Ed.), *The concept of activity in Soviet psychology* (pp. 37–71). Armonk, NY: M.E. Sharpe, Inc.

Minick, N., Stone, C. A., & Forman, E. (1993). Introduction: Integration of individual, social, and institutional processes in accounts of children's learning and development. In Forman, E., Minick, N., & Stone, C. A., *Contexts for learning* (pp. 3–16). New York: Oxford University Press.

Morris, D., Bloodgood, J. W., Lomax, R. G, & Perney, J. (2003). Developmental steps in learning to read: A longitudinal study in kindergarten and first grade. *Reading Research Quarterly, 38*(3), 302–323.

National Association for the Education of Young Children. (1998). Learning to read and write: Developmentally appropriate practices for young children. Joint position statement of the International Reading Association (IRA) and the *National Association for the Education of Young Children (NAEYC), 53*(4), 30–46.

National Reading Panel. (2000). *Teaching children to read.* Jessup, MD: Education Publications Center.

Rogoff, B., Mosier, C., Mistry, J, & Göncü, A. (1993). Toddlers' guided participation in a cultural activity. In E. Forman, N. Minick, & C. A. Stone, *Contexts for learning* (pp. 230–253). New York: Oxford University Press.

Snow, C. E., Burns, M. S., & Griffin, P. (Eds.) (1998). National Research Council. *Preventing reading difficulties in young children.* Washington, DC: National Academy Press.

Showers, B. (1990). Aiming for superior classroom instruction for all children: A comprehensive staff development model. *Remedial and Special Education, 11*(3), 35–39.

Shulman, L. S. (1986). Those who understand: Knowledge growth in teaching. *Educational Researcher, 15*(2), 4–14.

Teale, W., & Sulzby, E . (1989). Emerging literacy: New perspectives. In D. Strickland & L. Morrow, *Emerging literacy: Young children learn to read and write.* Newark, DE: International Reading Association.

Vygotsky, L. S. (1978). *Mind in society.* Cambridge, Massachusetts: Harvard University Press.

Wertsch, J. V. (1998). *Mind as action.* New York: Oxford University Press.

Zeichner, K. M. & Liston, D. P. (1996). *Reflective teaching: An introduction.* Mahwah, New Jersey: Lawrence Erlbaum Associates.

Index

adult roles in the classroom (ARIC), 113
analysis and strategy, 46

Berry Brazelton, 23
book planning, 58
book reading, 60

CCAC, 110
Center for Improvement of Early
   Reading Achievement (CIERA), 91
CCSAR, 111–15, 116
Connecticut Charts-A-Course, 12, 110
CCAC, 110, 113, 114, 128, 131
cognitive neuroscience, 20
Connecticut's Blueprint for Reading
   Achievement, 108, 109
Connecticut State Department of
   Education, 108
Connie Kamii, 18

Dave Weikert, 18
David Dickinson, 34
Dewey, 93
developmental supervision, 43, 47

early childhood environment, 20
early language and literacy classroom
   observation, 33

EDC, 109, 112
ELLCO, 33–39, 112, 113, 129
emergent writing, 55

Good Night Moon, 26

Hart and Risley, 16
How Are the Children? Report on Early
   Childhood Development and
   Learning, 24–25
high scope, 18
higher faculty institute survey, 113
home environments, 17

International Reading Association, 6
IRA, 6

LEEP, 33, 88, 109, 114, 126, 127
literacy, language and curriculum belief
   and practices of preschool teachers,
   112, 131
literacy training index, 113

meaningful differences, 16
Montessori, 18–20

National Association for the Education
   of Young Children, 6

NAEYC, 6–7
National Research Council, 6
No Child Left Behind, 82

Observation, 46

PELD, 112, 120–25
perry preschool project, 18
phonological awareness, 51
practical-argument staff development (PASD), 94
pre-observation conference, 46
professional development, 82, 83, 94
project STARS, 9–10, 33, 108–10, 141
peabody picture vocabulary test, 111, 118
pedagogical content knowledge (PCK), 90
post-conference analysis, 46
Public Act 97-259, 16
PPVT, 111, 114, 118, 126, 127

Reggio Emilia, 19
Report on early childhood development & learning, 27

scaffolding, 71
school readiness, 5
SERC, 110–11, 113
social-emotional development, 71
Special Education Resource Center, 110
striving to achieve reading success, 1
success for all, 89
supervision, 43
supervisory conference, 46
supervisory practices and attitudes, 112

The Boy Who Would Be a Helicopter, 78

Vygotsky, 16

White House Summit on Early Childhood Cognitive Development, 28

www.ingramcontent.com/pod-product-compliance
Lightning Source LLC
Chambersburg PA
CBHW030115010526
44116CB00005B/250